In the Weeds:

Navigating Student & Route Management

In the Weeds: Navigating Student & Route Management

For more information, email
sonia.mastros@busboss.com.

ISBN: 9798510190243
Imprint: Independently Published

GET YOUR FREE GIFT!

To get the best experience with this book, I've found readers who download and use our BusBoss Planner are able to implement faster and take the next steps needed to get the most out of BusBoss.

You will get a FREE copy when you purchase our BusBoss School Bus Routing Software Solution.

Table of Contents

Preface

If you work with routing students, you have been there – deep in the weeds. Some days it feels like we may never get out, but we here at BusBoss want you to know you are not alone, we understand your obstacles, we have experienced your frustration, and we have absolutely found solutions. This book is about our experiences with routing and the different ways we have helped our clients. The tips, tricks, skills, and insights we have gained along the way of our journey can be found within its pages.

The team members at BusBoss (Orbit Software) have documented their individual experiences, trials, and successes for you, our reader. We want you to be successful, no matter if this is your first time dealing with bus routing or if you have been doing this for years. So, take a look inside and we will walk with you and help navigate you through the challenging, sometimes monumental, but always fulfilling job of routing students.

Foreword

Have you ever been interested in learning more about managing school bus routes? This book is not only a helpful guide for like-minded professionals, but also a story of how BusBoss became what it is today. Not only will you learn valuable skills on how to successfully manage your own routes, but you will also gain exclusive insight into how school routing software works.

INTRODUCTION

Sonia Mastros
"Golf Goddess"

BusBoss is Born!

It was November of 1997, the day when BusBoss owners Sonia and George Mastros decided to commit their vows to each other for the rest of their lives. For better or for worse is one of the key staples in not only their marriage, but also their business. With that being said, Sonia and George have always been leaders who have shared their own slices of the struggle pie. However, that doesn't mean that they never found their way out stronger than they were before.

When Sonia and George Mastros were considering their next business venture, they knew that they were going to utilize their passion for technology to create a software program that would help schools provide efficient, safe, and cost-effective school bus routing for their students. With this idea in mind, their main goal was to make sure all kids had sufficient transportation to and from school; leaving no child behind.

Through the power of automating the process, nothing was ever left to chance. Sonia and George knew that the old way of creating maps with the pin-and-string method no longer served as an acceptable management tool. Since manual bus routing takes months on average to create, as well as a lack of viability for true optimization, tons of money and time was wasted. This resulted in school programs being eliminated due to a lack of innovation. Their philosophy was if they could save one teacher's position, keep music in schools, and sports or other programs running successfully, it was worth developing a bus routing system that helped school districts save time and money. In doing so, this would bring joy to the districts and their students.

After working in the industry for over 22 years, George Mastros has been awarded the Microsoft MVP Award seven times for his exceptional leadership and knowledge in the SQL server technical community. After developing software applications for the Department of Defense, he has moved on into the private sector where he delivers revolutionary technical solutions that solve large-scale problems.

Sonia Mastros has a multi-decade work history of partnering with school districts to develop a sophisticated school bus routing software program that optimizes bus routes, improves student safety, and increases parent satisfaction. She has been involved with BusBoss since the late 1990's and has been responsible for overseeing projects across various levels, ranging from large urban and suburban districts to smaller rural districts across the country. Her passion for improving transportation operations has not gone unnoticed.

George and Sonia have backed their dynamic, multifaceted software, BusBoss, with superb service, exceptional program prices, expert technical knowledge, and prompt turnaround times.

While reading this book and guide, you will discover that George and Sonia did not make BusBoss successful on their own. In fact, you will be hearing from their experienced staff, because without them, they would not have made this all possible.

While reading, you will hear personal stories from each member on their team, the struggles followed by the successes. More importantly, you will learn that they did not sit and wait for the right moment to come. They hustled to make the change happen.

GETTING STARTED
Learning the Industry

Daisy Oliveras
"World's Worst Assistant"

"I didn't know how to speak English"

I've been working at Orbit Software since 2010. After finishing my bachelor's degree in accounting, I moved to Pennsylvania from Puerto Rico and started working at Orbit Software. I didn't know how to speak English, but Sonia still gave me the opportunity to work at her company. Now years later, I'm also the Office Manager and Bookkeeper for the entire company. I'm also in charge of gathering and planning for Trade Shows, sales presentations, and preparation for before, during, and after shows.

My first assignment at Orbit Software was creating the BusBoss booklets as handouts to the trade show attendees. The Booklet contains information about our products and our contact information. The BusBoss Booklet is a 6 X 9 book, so it is quite easy to carry with you. When you want to promote your product at a tradeshow, you should keep in mind that most of the time the attendees are traveling and they don't want to have bulky stuff to carry around and take home, unless it is a TV, they won at a raffle drawing.

Trade Show Registration

Trade Shows are a fun and great way to learn about the industry and advertise your product. If you decide to go to a trade show, first, you have to register. During the registration process, they offer different ways to advertise your products. For example, bag inserts. We like providing the bag inserts because we can make it fun for the potential client. On the flyer, we advertise our product and make a game out of it. At one of the trade shows, we were giving away an Echo Show as a prize, and the attendees would have to tell us our AKA (also known as) name which they could find on the flyer. Mine was "World's Worst Assistant" and Sonia's was "Golf Goddess". It was fun trying to make them say that I was the "World's Worst Assistant" and at the same time, it would help break the ice.

If you are a vendor, you are able to select a Sponsorship to advertise your product, putting your company out there. Each trade show is unique, and they have different ways of how each operates. Some trade shows have different levels of sponsorships. Some sponsorships offer to put door hangers at each attendee's room with your product information and your booth number for them to come and visit you. Sometimes you can also have signs around the conference floor advertising your product. Others do tournaments, like golf or bowling, where they advertise your company throughout the event. This is a good way to have fun while working!

Sometimes you will have the opportunity to be in a panel. When you are in a panel, you are able to present your points of view and also learn more about the attendees needs. During the conference, they have classes scheduled for each of the members. You should assist at some of them because you will be able to learn more about their needs and how your product can help them.

Another way of advertising is by hosting a meet and greet. We found the best way is to rent a bigger room while providing food and drinks. This will give the attendees a chance to unwind and relax from the busy conference environment. Doing so, you are giving them the opportunity to know you and your product, but in a friendly manner.

Pre-Show

Besides registering and advertising, you need to plan. Making a checklist can help you organize the trade show, making sure you stay on top of everything. Sometimes, you will need to fly to another state and get a hotel or even rent a car. One thing we always check if we are staying at a hotel is if the hotel provides a shuttle. This allows us to save money so we wouldn't need to rent a car. Uber is a great way to get around without having to deal with paying tolls. Another thing to think about is what is included with the booth. Renting electronics can be really expensive. What we do is that we buy a TV and use it to show our software. At the end of the trade show, we give it away as a prize. You pay less by buying the TV instead of renting it and the attendees are happy because they can win a TV. Make sure to take all the cables needed for it, which you will list on your checklist. On the checklist, you can list things like Registration, Airfare Reservation, Hotel Reservation, Car Rental Reservation, Electronics, cables, all of the Marketing Materials, with quantities of each, raffle prizes and giveaways etc.

Besides all of the marketing materials like the BusBoss Enterprise Flyer, the BusBoss Portfolio, or even our DISTRICTpatrol Flyer, we even take old business cards as well. Sometimes, the attendees don't have theirs so they will use ours to write their information on the back, so we can contact them later for a software demonstration.

Before the show, you will receive an email from the trade show hosting company. This email will include an attachment with the pre-attendee list including the attendees email addresses. We use this list to send an email blast to the attendees to invite them to our booth. We will also write some information about our product and mention our raffle. For the raffle, we don't ask for a business card. Instead, we use raffle tickets. That way they don't feel pressure that someone will be calling them.

During the Show

During the show, we try to get the attendees attention by offering a raffle ticket for the big prize giveaway. Besides the raffle prize, we hand out other giveaways which we use to advertise BusBoss. As an example, we give them a hand sanitizer spray. They can put it in their packet and take it anywhere. We imprint our logo and slogan on the giveaways to advertise our products.

Using giveaways draws attendees to our booth to then give us the opportunity to show them a little bit of our Routing and Scheduling Software. Attendees like to "Trick or Treat", so this is a way you can get them to talk to you. You can have candy or something small that will get their attention. As an example, we have given out laptop camera shields. We have also given away wine glasses. Attendees loved them. They would let others know and actually bring them to our booth.

This is when we show them how our products are different. We show them our mapping and geocoding functionality and how easy it is to move stops from one point to another without changing any student. We also show them how to easily make changes on a route, how to add a street on the map and how to generate State Reports, which are really beneficial for them. After we briefly show them our software, we ask if they would like to schedule a live demonstration where we can show our product in greater detail and how we can help them.

Another good way to get to know more about the attendees and their needs is by attending classes. During these classes you will not only learn about the industry but also hear from the attendees directly. Also plan on mingling with them at the show or at a pre-scheduled get-together. During the get-together, you can talk to them to hear about their concerns and issues you may be able to resolve. In doing so, you build a rapport by helping them, so they start to feel confident with you and your products.

After the Show

A day or two after the trade show, Nicholas Ferrante will follow-up with them to schedule a demonstration. The follow-up is really important to do while it is fresh in the attendees' mind because they can forget since they see so many vendors. Make sure to have or do something that impresses them, that way when you call to schedule the demonstration, they will know who they are talking to and why it is important for them to attend the demo.

Chapter Recap

- Trade Show Vendor Options!

    o   Sponsorships
    o   Bag Inserts
    o   Classes
    o   Host a Meet & Greet

- Attendee Options

    o   Learn the Industry
    o   Attend Classes
    o   Visit Booths
    o   Schedule Follow-ups
    o   Enter Raffles & Win Prizes

SO MANY CHOICES
How to decide what program or process to use

Nicholas Ferrante
"Sasquatch"

Build a Relationship

This process starts with the first contact I have with the prospect. I am the main person responsible for speaking with anyone interested in BusBoss. My position is designed to be the action that leads to sales and revenue for the company. Selling any product can be a difficult prospect, but there are ways that we communicate with potential clients that end up helping me in my endeavors immensely.

Entering the hectic world of Student Transportation, the best advice that I can give is that every school is laboring under their own set of difficulties that they need to overcome. When first learning about school transportation, a major benefit for me was by attending trade shows; not just for the interactions with the individual members of many departments, but with the broadening of my understanding of some of the issues that come from trying to route a diverse slate of students.

Attending lectures during these trade shows, I learned about the difficulties with routing homeless students, struggles with driver retention, and the importance of special education routing. It is important to not only attend these trade shows and lectures, but to also use them to adapt your routing in a world of shifting priorities. I mention trade shows because it is an important part of building a relationship with a customer. By doing this, it helps us in understanding their position and empathizing with their challenges. Before I began attending trade shows, I had a limited idea of the scope of the complications involved in the seemingly simple task of transporting students from one location to another.

Some of the issues could reasonably be predicted, while I only found out about others because Sonia insisted that I sit in on presentations that ended up being extremely useful. Each new idea or more nuanced issue expanded my expectations when first interacting with clients and allowed me to better predict and adapt to their needs.

The beginning of the process, for me, is at the point of initial contact. This means of contact can come from many sources. Sometimes I only interact with an individual over the phone or other times I've already met them at a trade show. In either case, it is important to take notes after each interaction. Building the relationship can be as simple as being able to recite earlier comments or issues stated and by offering a solution without further prodding.

Showcasing your knowledge of the field and predicting issues that might come from their situation can also serve to set yourself up as an experienced member of your organization. This is something that was a struggle on my first day speaking with transportation directors and superintendents. Without a firm grasp on the functionality and adaptability of your product, you risk losing the confidence that individual might have had in being able to offer them a solution to their problems. Once the initial contact has been concluded, it is important to move them towards the next step in the process, the demo.

The relationship with a school district begins with the first exposure to the name of your company and any reputation held by those close with the potential prospect. You need to understand that in some situations, the prospect has an ironclad opinion of your product. A huge part of being able to sell products in general is by convincing the individual that the service you are offering will solve their problem. On the opposite side of this discussion, for any schools looking to get transportation software, there isn't much information on any of the programs you might end up using. In this case, my recommendation would be asking other schools in your area. There have been many instances where I felt that individuals attending the demo were viewing each function I mentioned as if they were shocked that it was an option. For both the salesman and the customer, the more informed you both are about the needs of the client, the more likely it is that each person will be satisfied with the product.

Software Demonstration

The demo for BusBoss is intended to be a broad coverage of all of the concerns or issues that the transportation department might have about their current state of affairs. The pre-demo survey that we send out with every demo confirmation is key to helping us narrow the scope of the demo to better suit the needs of each school district, day care, summer camp, or contractor. The pre-demo survey is a useful tool to allow us to glean any information or any problems to which we could act as a solution. Sometimes school districts only see the surface problems without delving deeper into the root of the issue. This is where the combination of being able to think and react quickly becomes even more important. The demo itself is a blanket that is meant to cover or allow for coverage of any number of issues currently hounding their district. The purpose of your own intuitiveness, along with any additional info found in the pre-demo survey, is to put more pressure on highlighted issues with the individual that you are currently dealing with. Being proactive and addressing the issues before they are mentioned or using the notes you took to highlight smaller concerns that may have seemed trivial at the time, will all serve to build a better relationship. In doing so, this helps you get closer to the sale. The demo is where the majority of your focused interaction will come from and it should act as the last step to move them from indecision to clarity. The conversation almost never ends with the demo however, and all of the work you've put in so far can disappear if you aren't attentive to the needs of the school district.

Most school districts require additional confirmations to be able to make an important decision like the purchase of routing software. This can add up to days and even weeks during which there is little to no change in the likelihood of the sale. During this time, it is critical that you keep your product in the mind of the school district. It is not enough that they reacted positively with the demo, they need to think about your product as their *solution*. It requires a fine balance to be able to make sure you aren't overeager, as I was early in my time with Orbit Software. Make sure you are available and prompt with any questions or concerns coming from your contact. The relationship needs to be maintained and the good qualities of your software can be further reinforced. Understanding the situation, the associated costs for the software, and what the correct choice for that district might be. We also make sure that our prospects understand that we are available and willing to discuss our software. For some of these schools, purchasing immediately is not going to be an option. In these cases, it is important to leave a lasting impact. When they are ready to move on from their current product, they should immediately be thinking of BusBoss. Once the prospect hits the tipping point, make sure you are readily available if there are a whole host of new questions. Most school districts need to pass any purchase through their school board before purchases can be made and this can result in a slate of questions from a completely different perspective. If you have done your job well and educated your contact on the possibilities of BusBoss, this process should go by smoothly. It is good to think of your job as making sure that the people you speak to have the necessary information to make the best choice based on their needs.

Knowledge of the product is key to building a good experience around viewing the software. In the school's position, what are their needs and what are their wants? Would BusBoss Pro be a better fit for them, or do they need one of our add-ons? Do they have issues with keeping track of their vehicles? Then they might want a demo more focused on TRIPpatrol, our GPS tracking software. Do they have issues with students getting on the wrong bus? A demo of STUDENTpatrol and a focus on methods of better managing student locations would be appropriate. iBusBoss would be used for better, and easier, communication with parents. MyTRIPS for field trip management. We have a variety of products and accessories available that might be exactly what they need. Each demo can be tailored to the needs of the individual school district or contractor. These demos allow me to show off some of the better features of the program along with giving me an opportunity to counter any concerns and answer any questions that the prospect may have. The demo, for us here at BusBoss, is an incredibly important first step in moving forward with the sale.

The demo is the opportunity to showcase your product, making sure the prospect is aware of all of the ways that your program can help them meet their needs. Use the information you have gained through the pre-demo survey, previous contact, and your own intuition. BusBoss, for example, has a few functions that we make sure are mentioned in every demo. We really like to talk about concerns that we've seen school districts really struggle with adapting to in their normal operations. Having a further understanding of how helpful and easily accessed our support functions are can also help bridge the gap. Not only will we train you on our product, but we also stick with you through learning the program you just purchased. Convincing the individual that your product will be worth the expense, solidifies that they believe in their return on investment, going a long way towards landing the sale.

An early lesson in working with our form of software is trying to match what the prospect might be expecting. There are many different ways that expectations can be altered by sources outside your control. Sometimes it's as simple as having a close relationship with a sister school that can afford student tracking, or I've even seen the parents of students reach out to us for demos trying to force the school to make an adjustment. It can be difficult to notice all of these external factors, but it is still important when trying to match the individual to the product that will work best for them in their situation. Make sure they understand what they are buying and the ways in which our product can help them achieve their goals; give them an understanding of both the up-front costs as well as the year-to-year cost, helping them decide if they would benefit better from purchasing or renting. This is also going to help them better decide whether you are the right choice for them to make to meet their needs.

Another important lesson I learned pertaining to prospect satisfaction was the importance of note taking. Keeping track of questions asked, comments made, and concerns can all help to build a better picture of the goals of that department. This can also serve as a list of items that should be covered in the demo. The pre-demo survey is immensely helpful, but not everyone has the time or the patience to fill one out, hence the continued need for thorough note taking. The demo should act as a culmination of all of the information that has been gleaned. Each point that you noted as being important to the client must be addressed. Once the demo is completed, you need to keep your product at the forefront. Be prompt, be confident, and make sure to use your knowledge and confidence in your product to make the prospect feel they are making the best decision possible. Building a relationship with the individual is a great way to open new doors and build a better basis from which to work when trying to make the sale.

After this step in the process, hopefully they have made a choice to begin using BusBoss. And, if you have done a thorough job, they will move into implementation.

Chapter Recap

- Did you see anything you think might work for you?

    - What features and functionality are important to you?
    - Is the Quality or Cost of Product and Customer Support the most important?
    - What are the associated Costs (Initial & Future)?
    - How long to recoup your costs (ROI)?

- Is continuing with what you have already a viable option?

    - What are the Pros &

IMPLEMENTING ROUTING SOFTWARE
Decision to purchase software has been made, now what?

James Kulp
"V.P. of Sarcasm"

Data Collect and Analysis

Data collection is primarily centered around the data being submitted by the client. Part of our standard data and route conversion process involves reviewing the data submitted and ensuring that it is in a format that we can load it into the software. This often means analyzing and cleaning the data, for example, removing bad characters, spacing, abbreviations, etc., along with reviewing it for missing data. We are also checking for duplicated data or data that is not logical in the context provided.

If we find issues, we will often need to reach back out to the client for clarifications, corrections, editions, and deletions.

"Commit to Getting it Done"

Is the advice I will often give to the client up front. Yes, it is a bit time consuming in the beginning, but once it's put all together in a timely fashion, the process is much smoother. There will be a lot of back and forth between the implementation specialist and the client. Questions regarding the data being submitted, clarifications, and trying to understand the way things work with each individual client is commonplace. Therefore, it will take some commitment on both the client side and the specialist side to push through and work together. This way, it helps bring the information that is needed and present it in a way that makes sense.

Drop Dead Deadlines

I am not really sure why they call it that except that it tends to keep everyone on the same page. Having a schedule allows everyone to focus better and understand more clearly what needs to be submitted and when.

One of our greatest selling points is a quick turnaround time. We advise the client that as long as they submit the data on schedule, we can complete the data and route conversion and get them up and running within four weeks.

This is a broad example of our 30-day planned implementation timeline:

Week 1

- New order Processing
- Reference and planning - Kick Off meeting with Client
- Start of Data submission
- Database Setup and Map preparation

Week 2

- Data submission - questions and answers
- Data conversion and loading

Week 3

- Route conversion and loading route data
- Map address and stop geocoding
- Route verifications
- Pre-installation steps

Week 4

- Installation
- Training
- Support

However, even with a schedule in place, the unexpected can occur. What I mean is that different scenarios can happen and keeping a project on schedule can be a challenge, even under ideal conditions. I have worked with many customers that are juggling multiple job responsibilities, not only working in transportation, but may be in charge of maintenance, cafeteria, administration, etc.

Another factor that can help or hurt the deadline is whether we need to involve multiple people in the process. You know what they say about too many cooks in the kitchen. Well, the same holds true here. A good example is when I am working with a transportation person along with a business administrator, and a technical support representative. In some cases, this simply can't be avoided. Each person brings a different skill set that is needed to the project. However, in my experience, it also tends to slow things down simply because you have several people who all need to communicate with one another to keep the project running smoothly.

With all of our clients, we attempt to foster clear communication and teamwork. We are all working together to complete the project on schedule. At the end of the day, the schedule is determined by the client. With their responsibilities and priorities, we work and guide them along in the process. The goal is getting them up and running as soon as we can.

Metrics and KPIs

BusBoss has built-in functionality for metrics and KPI's. This can be found under the BusBoss Benchmarks, which provides a grade for industry standard KPIs such as the average age of your fleet, the percentage of spare buses, your daily seat usage, the average ride time per day, bus usage, cost per bus per day, cost per rider per day, and cost per mile operated.

Part of our A+ software checkpoints have an associate contacting the client after the 1st 180 days in order to review the Benchmarks with them. They also oversee how the client has progressed since the installation date.

Software Implementation

As part of the software implementation process, we are with you every step of the way. We work with you and guide you along such as assisting with collecting data, interpreting the way that you are currently doing your routing, and how we can transform your data into useful information that can be loaded into the software to reflect the way that you run those routes. Along the way, we answer questions, deal with any issues that may crop up, and act as an advocate on your behalf.

The goal of a software implementation specialist is to get you up and running as quickly as possible. During this process, we want to ensure that you understand how to use the software, make sure that communication between everyone works well, and to foster an ongoing relationship. After you are set up and trained on the software, that relationship continues as a support system for you and your staff.

Stay Up-to-Date

You have been installed, the transportation staff has undergone training, and you are actively using the program! Congrats, that's awesome!

The final piece for you to consider and keep in mind after the initial installation and training is the ongoing support and maintenance. Having an active and ongoing support contract means you have access to:

- Client Support Representatives anytime you have a question or issue.

- Automatic updates to the software when you login to BusBoss.

- Access to the Support Forum – programs which allows you to post questions and download any of the items purchased by your company.

Many times, this final piece of the puzzle is overlooked. However, it is an important piece and should definitely be included to alleviate any issues you have in the future. Our support staff are meticulously trained on the ins and outs of BusBoss. They not only know the software, but also have a technical background that allows them to troubleshoot a variety of issues. As you will see below, they take pride in the job they do and enjoy fostering and building ongoing relationships between our team and yours.

Onboarding and Mentoring

One of the items I consider to be of the highest importance is onboarding and mentoring new associates. I have been the new person often enough to say with certainty that it is highly stressful. You have doubts going in, you may be thinking to yourself, am I going to fit in here? Can I do the job? Will they like me? Will I like them? and several others.

I know from experience that when I am starting a new job, starting a new process, heck starting anything new, it is much less stressful if I understand what the expectations are. In doing so, I have a way to ensure that I am achieving those expectations. In a brand-new environment or situation where I am expected to learn new material, my stress is greatly reduced if there is a formal training process that I can work through. In this case, it should allow me to provide feedback as to how I am processing the information.

I also believe in the importance of ongoing training and mentoring. Ongoing training is essential in staying current with a rapidly changing environment; making sure you are providing the best support possible. Along those lines, I encourage the use of a mentor or training buddy, specifically someone with a high level of experience and knowledge.

Everyone is a Customer

I start my day with the knowledge that literally everyone I deal with on a daily basis is a customer. Whether I am interacting with vendors, client's, co-workers, or the management team at OSI, I treat them all as customers. In doing so, I treat each person with respect. I actively listen to what they are saying and respond in a way that is intended to be beneficial to them or the situation they describe.

A large part of my daily activity is listening and accurately interpreting what is being communicated. This often means asking clarifying probing questions, restating, or paraphrasing the person's most important thoughts to ensure that I fully understand what is being communicated. I believe in order to be successful in a customer service environment like ours, developing good communications skills are essential. Clients are not calling to shoot the breeze and catch up with you. They are calling because there is a problem, which means they are most likely already stressed out and annoyed. In the customer service field, it is our job to listen, understand, and help resolve the issue to the client's satisfaction.

I do this by being courteous and listening to each client. I may need to ask a few questions to fully understand the issue, but only after I have given them the time to vent and voice their frustrations, I am able to help fix the conflict.

I recall a situation in which the client indicated that he was used to using another software program and that ours is one that did not make much sense to him. In retrospect, every function he did not understand in the program annoyed him; thus, thinking that it was an annoyance. In his mind, our system was broken or inferior.

During the call, I just listened and as the client continued to speak, he slowly became calmer and started making statements like "okay I see how this is working now" and " I guess this is okay."

During the call, I encouraged him to show me the items that he was having issues with and then I walked him through how to use that function, sometimes two or three times. Afterwards, I would ask him to give it a try. When it worked for him, I could hear the relief in his voice and the stress starting to melt away. By the end of the call, the client had resolved his immediate issues and gained a better understanding of the way the software worked. My best advice here would be to go in with an open mind and to think like a customer when dealing with a client. How would you want to be spoken to if you were in their shoes?

Maintain Some Type of Personal and Work Balance

Of course, I want to do a good job. I have a sense of pride and accomplishment when I come home at the end of a day knowing that I had given it my all. The same passion and commitment I bring to work, I also bring to my personal life.

Sometimes I have to ask myself, or I should say remind myself, "Why am I working?" Well, it is to make a better life for my family and myself; to have the means to provide. However, if all of my time is spent in that pursuit and I have no time to enjoy the fruit of my labors, then it's pointless. The point that I'm trying to make is that you have to have some type of work-life balance. You don't want to be a workaholic. Some specific advice: limit your workday to no more than 10-12 hours. Afterwards, spend some time with your family and live your life!

"Happy wife, happy life" is a quote that I use to joke around with when I am with married friends. Working in the industry, like being in a marriage, you will need to know how to compromise, take criticism, and find solutions. You not only need to have some thick skin to redirect anger and rejection, but you also need to know how to be quick thinking, open of opinions from others, and to be able to think not only in the designated parameters but beyond them as well. There has been many a time that I was assigned a project thinking that it was going to be simple process, but in reality, getting into the thick of it all with a customer being very frustrated. But this is the reason I enjoy this position; being given the chance to take a concept we have already planned out and understanding what is wrong with the current design. In doing so, we can find a solution or even come up with new ideas to meet the expected outcome for a client. I see this as a 1000-piece puzzle and I know I need to figure out what pieces connect, making the image come together in the end.

For our associates and our customers, I try to be a mentor. I am the person that will share my experience and knowledge. I will guide them through the process ensuring that they are comfortable with the process. In doing this, they become knowledgeable and have the tools and skills that they need to be confident moving forward.

STUDENT INFORMATION SYSTEMS INTEGRATION

Sean Long
"Grumpy Bear"

The Ever-Evolving World of Technology and how to have it work for you.

There are multiple ways to name or call something within the English language; it all depends on what region of the world or cultural background you come from. What I call an apartment, my friend in England may call a loft. The trunk of a car may be called a boot by others. When you get an Italian sandwich from a deli, do you call it a hoagie or a sub? Working with different computer database systems and customers is no different.

Although there are similarities to the tools that are used to get results, each company may have their own data structures which make them unique. Because of this, one needs to be flexible and adjust to the ever-changing environments. They must be able to think outside the box to find solutions to different problems and ask for guidance and help from others when it is needed.

Hello, my name is Sean, and I am one of the Data Analysts and Software Developers for Orbit Software, makers of BusBoss. When I first thought of data analysis, I pictured sheets upon sheets of Excel spreadsheets, screens of data, and trying to find that one number that has an incorrect decimal place which is throwing off my department's annual budget reports. When in reality, the majority of my work is asking a customer what information they want added or modified in our software and digging through data and code to find a solution.

The job can be seen as a maze you would see in comics or newspapers. You know the entrance and are able to see the exit marked on the map, but you need to maneuver through the maze of twisting corridors and dead ends to get to the exit. Sometimes traversing the maze is as simple as a few keystrokes to get to the end, while other times, the correct path to the end is obscured or met with multiple obstacles. A Data Analyst needs to take these challenges head on; think outside the box and find the best path to reach the end. While the journey is hard at times, in the end, the sense of accomplishment is worth the journey.

One of the tools used in this role is SQL Server Management Studio, or a similar integrated environments used to manage databases. This allows me to send requests to a database and gather results which will help me determine the best course of actions to properly get the end results for our customers.

The next tool I use a lot is SQL Profiler. This tool allows me to audit what SQL cues a program is calling from our SQL databases. This helps me understand how an existing software tool works and assists me with troubleshooting errors which may be occurring when the software runs due to unexpected or bad information being passed. The next tools I use are different Development Environment Suites such as Visual Studio, Eclipse, or Inno Setup. With these systems, I am able to create the complex procedures which processes the requested data, thus producing the results our customers are looking for. The last tools in my arsenal are community boards, internet searches, and peer guidance. When you meet a hurdle and you can't find an immediate solution, just researching what others have done to overcome a similar situation can bring new ideas to view and help.

One of the many data integration programs we offer are Custom Import and Export Tools. The end results of these tools are to allow a company to set up a data transfer routine between our products and another database. These tools in particular keep track of Student information. Our tool is designed specifically around how the Student Information System manages data. This means that I will need to understand how information is stored in our customer's student information system, what information will be provided to me, and what information is expected from BusBoss. Data consistency is important when you need to send information across multiple companies and users. You need to be aware of how data is being used and how it can affect operations if it is not in the correct format or when it isn't being sent properly.

Data consistency is important when it comes to managing a database-backed application as well. Having consistent data will help with keeping the information organized and allow users to find and maintain data. In doing so, this helps to improve productivity and output within the workplace. Having consistency allows users to more easily group data together to provide useful reports such as student school assignments, emergency contact lists, and transportation schedules. Making sure you keep data constant in your database system will also make it easier for other applications or companies to process data you provide them as well. Although other companies may have a different way of storing data, having consistent data will make it easier for them to develop ways to manage the data which is provided to them.

How data is provided across systems is something a Data Analyst also needs to be aware of. Since no two databases are exactly alike, it is common to find similar data to be handled and stored differently across systems. Developers need to understand this. They also need to be willing to work with each other when it comes to sending and retrieving data from each other's databases. In BusBoss, we allow students to have multiple different route assignments and take into consideration split-custody situations, which may mean a student being on a different routes on different days. Because of this, BusBoss stores student route assignments paired with a weekday and purpose (ten am and ten pm records). Through this setup, we are able to provide unique routing situations throughout the course of the week instead of being limited to one or two routes per student. Another vendor who focuses more on school progression for a student may also wish to keep track of student busing assignments, but instead of being able to show an assignment for each day and purpose, they are only able to show one routing record for the student in the database. Also, the routing data from that student system, could then be used to send a daily routine report to all the parents informing them when and where the bus will pick-up their student.

Along the way, an Analyst may encounter a multitude of obstacles which will risk the project's completion and will have them pulling their hair out. Luckily, if we have encountered an issue, it is a good possibility that someone else has as well whether it be a co-worker, boss, other IT professionals, or the 5th-grade computer teacher in Reykjavik. Seeking help from others when you reach a hurdle is nothing to be ashamed of. In actuality, it's usually a good thing. There have been many times when I was stuck on a hurdle in code, just spinning my wheels and getting nowhere, so I would reach out to a superior for some guidance or suggestions on how they would tackle this situation. Being able to step back, look at the situation, and listen to how someone else would handle the situation, is a crucial quality to have when dealing with Data Analytics. From seeking the help needed, you only better yourself by learning from others. This in turn will help the company grow in the direction we all want to go. Computer Programming is an ever-expanding field of work where new theories and concepts are being created on a daily basis, which makes it hard to know everything there is about every computer language. But by speaking to other professionals and sharing experiences, you can only grow more knowledgeable.

With the pace of how the world is becoming more technically savvy and new programming ideas are being developed by the day, it is crucial for technicians to constantly build their knowledge base and grow. When companies allow employees the time and support to learn new concepts, the business as a whole will also prosper. With more knowledge and training under their belts, the technicians would be able to put into practice what they have learned; having a better knowledge of the tools they are using.

This means they are able to create solutions and new projects faster, which also leads them to being able to support more customers and allowing shorter turnaround times of new projects for increased revenue.

Besides a normal classroom or webinar environment, there are a plethora of websites, blogs, and forums which like-minded thinkers gather to talk about programming concepts. Just by reading how someone else overcame a similar issue can educate you on how to handle getting over the hurdle you are encountering; sparking enough imagination to find the solution and overcoming the issue.

I find the 3 main websites that I am on constantly is W3Schools, Stack Overflow, and Microsoft Help forums. If I cannot find my solutions there, I can go to the Search browser and look for any other articles on the issues I am having.

Once a new report, integration tool or program functionality is completed, it needs to be tested thoroughly to discover if there are any issues or bugs still present with the product. Once going through development and final testing, the product is ready to be released. Afterwards, it becomes time to train the front lines operatives who will be entrusted with helping the current and future BusBoss users. These front-line operatives are our friendly customer relations support staff who are there to help answer any questions or help solve any troubling issues a user may be encountering.

Chapter Recap

- Commit to getting it done!

- Expected implementation timeline

- Lots of time has gone into making this decision, things to plan on.

  - Data Analysis, Dealing with the Unexpected
  - Drop Dead Deadlines
  - Metrics and KPIs
  - Staff Onboarding
  - Software Implementation

- Stay up to date with software support and maintenance

SOFTWARE SUPPORT & MAINTENANCE
Getting Help & Updates when you need them

Heather Filer
"Crazy Yarn Lady"

"Thank you for calling Orbit, this is Heather, how may I help you?"

Starting with that simple sentence, I go from mild-mannered, average techie to "Super Support Extraordinaire!" And it is all thanks to a great little/big company that gave me a chance to reinvent my career.

Before starting with Orbit Software, the makers of BusBoss, I had been out of work for a little over a year. The company I had been with for 16-plus years had a layoff – and I was one of many affected. With so much time on my hands, I decided that a career change was in order. So, I took online classes at a computer school and not only passed all the classes but earned *eight* IT certifications.

I applied to different companies for about three months before I found Orbit Software on LinkedIn. I applied and the rest is history. Not only was I extremely impressed with the sophisticated products they offered at the time, and the fact I would be working with data and proprietary software, but I was drawn to the family environment the company fostered. They were willing to give me a chance – someone fresh to the IT world and in the process of changing careers later in life. So, grab a cup of coffee with me, and I'll tell you all about what I do.

My day really does start with a cup of coffee, otherwise I can't form a complete sentence! And that is important because I am at the frontlines for customer support. I can't express how much satisfaction I get from knowing that I am not only helping our clients, but I am helping my co-workers. Because we are so small, we all wear multiple hats and have various responsibilities. When I was hired, it allowed the other members of the IT team to focus on the Tier 2 and Tier 3 levels of customer support. I am also able to give them one more person in the new client setup rotation. I may have been the new "low-woman" on the totem pole, but I've always known that I am an integral part of the day-to-day. Everyone has always treated me with respect, equality, and like another member of the family.

We have an IT meeting every morning to go over what we are working on, what issues we ran into during the previous day, how we solved them, and/or ask the group for help. It is also a great way to connect personally. This helped so much to have a connection during COVID when we all worked remotely. We share more than just work stuff in these meetings. We ask about family, we talk about the next social gathering, we kibitz, we laugh; we connect. It was very evident early on that this group of people were not just co-workers, they were a wonderfully diverse and crazy family. And they opened their arms wide to me.

The Ins and Outs of Customer Relationships

Another great thing about working for Orbit is that every day is a little different. It's not just support calls all day. There are usually two to five projects to work on, new clients to on-board, researching a particularly stubborn support issue, managing a client's data, or helping a fellow employee with their workload. There is never a dull moment working at Orbit!

Special Needs Routing

One of my ongoing assignments is to help one of our clients with their Special Needs Student Routing. Special Needs can mean Special Ed, mobility challenged, or special programs.

I usually start by looking to see if the stops for these students need to be Right-Side Pickups, also called Door Side Pickup. This setting requires the bus to pick up the student only on the right side (or door side) of the street, which prevents the student from having to cross the street. This is an important safety feature that the BusBoss software has, so our clients don't have to think about which way the bus is being routed. If they have to, they can also go in and change it. This can be set by grade-level, by marking a street as hazardous, or by manual settings in the stop.

Next, I would make sure that the addresses are located correctly. Stops are determined by address locations, so accuracy is especially important. Sometimes they don't translate to the map correctly, so I need to go in and manually locate the address on the map. If the address is there, just simply moving the stop closer to the street allows for accurate routing. The home address and "stop" address do not have to be the same. Knowing this, I can successfully route a homeless student. Even though their address is not located, I can place them on a stop that is located so they can be routed to their school.

The student attending a Special Program can also mean special routing. The student may be attending a second school throughout the week, like for a vo-tech program, or they may even go to a different school one day a week for special classes. These special routes can take place at any time and can be set up outside of the student's normal schedule. First, I would check to see if a special route already exists that the student could be placed on. If yes, then I can simply add that student's stop to the route. If not, I would create the special route, making sure to put the student's stop on that route. Once that is done, I would add it to the student profile through second school, transfers, or special routes.

Look Out!

Oh, and of course, we have to keep an eye out for the "Traps"! If you handle student routing, you know what I mean! Those roads that are too small for large busses, the dead-end streets, the one-way traffic only during certain times of the day, roads without any sidewalks or margins, highways … you get the idea. Orbit gets the maps from a third-party, and most of the time they are very accurate. Sometimes, though, I need to go in and help a client mark a street as one way or add a road that is new. I can also show them how to mark a road as "hazardous" – this means that it's dangerous for the student, so they should not be walking to a bus stop or crossing the street to get on the bus. I can also mark streets as restricted – by height, by weight, or both and set turn restrictions at hard to make intersections. We've all seen the sign for Low Clearance on an overpass. With a simple setting, I can make sure the large busses are not routed that way, but also know that the vans and shorter busses can safely pass through.

New Doesn't Have to be Scary

I know all that sounds kind of simple yet complicated. And I'm not going to lie – it is. When I first started, I was overwhelmed by the versatile and robust nature of the BusBoss program. There is so much stuff to learn and knowing the software inside and out is integral to what I do, because if I don't know the software, I can't be effective when the client calls with questions. The great thing is that it was easy to learn.

Even though I technically work on only one thing at a time, I have multiple irons in the fire. I need to be able to seamlessly move from one to the next without losing too much "where am I?" time in between. Notes are extremely helpful with that. Orbit has created a project management website where we can keep track of projects and tasks that we are working on. I also keep a document on my computer in One Note for little things, and extra notes on tasks I am in the middle of. You can never journal too much!

I have to say, coming to work for Orbit Software was a huge career change for me that did present a few challenges. Not only was I stepping into a role that was almost brand new for me, but even the industry itself was new! This was the first time I was exposed to bus routing software. Once explained, I thought, "Well, duh, of course this is a need!" However, this isn't something you think about unless you need to. So, in retrospect, everything was new.

As someone who has never been exposed to routing busses, I had to hit the ground running and learn fast! Even though I never did it, BusBoss software made it easy to understand, and many of the features are intuitive. So even though I was learning while working with the software, I had questions. I had to get over any inhibitions I had about looking dumb for asking questions. I asked so many questions! I was so afraid of letting the client down!

That first week of support calls on my own was the most stressful week at work. There were more than a few times throughout the process, that I thought that I would never get it and never be effective. So, I embraced the fact that when you start something new, there will be bumps in the road and learning curves along the way. But by sticking to it and remaining confident, and with the help and support of my coworkers, I was able to successfully master the software and understand the industry. Being aware of – and using – the resources at my fingertips didn't hurt either.

We have a help desk folder on our network with solutions to common issues. We also have a chat feature so that any member of our team is only a text away, and we have our IT meeting in the morning to go over things together like I mentioned previously.

Once I learned how to use those , I was able to become an additional resource for the team that very quickly turned into a second family.

Don't Just Sit There! Use It !

Now that you have the software installed, don't just let it sit there! The first step in using it is knowing what you have at your fingertips, and it doesn't matter if you are familiar with the task at hand or brand new. I love that Orbit offers a few things to get you started and help keep you going.

Community Forum

I know that I love collaborating with my coworkers, and if you are like most people, you also look to someone with experience to get answers to questions. That is why I love support sites that offer more than just a FAQ page. Look for a community forum where users can talk, ask questions, and collaborate. Does the site have downloadables? Can you contact the company directly through the forum? What about extra training?

Give me a site with quick videos and clips on how to do something, and I am a happy camper! And yes, if you are wondering, BusBoss offers just such a place. It is really nice when you have not only the expertise of the software developers right there, but it adds so much value when you can talk to other industry experts. Maybe you are new and need some guidance, or maybe you have experience that you want to pass on so someone else can have a better learning curve.

As an added bonus, our technical and customer support staff are in there regularly to not only answer questions, but to look at what clients are saying; to get ideas on how we can improve on the customer experience. Don't forget to sign up!

Software Support and Training

And speaking of experience, how often have you been given a task, or gotten a new electronic device, and thought to yourself "If only there was someone to SHOW me how to use this!" Some new things can be daunting, but when you have someone who can walk you through the steps, they suddenly become so much clearer. Training is essential. We understand that. Any software worth their salt will offer instructor led training. And because everyone has a different learning curve, there should be different options - online or in person - and different lengths to cater to your needs. But what if you only have one quick question, you ask? We hear you! Being able to reach our Technical Customer Support quickly and easily in a variety of ways helps to ease stress and lessen worries. We offer a chat option, department email (so that your request does not go into an inbox that is on vacation or no longer valid), and phones answered by real live people.

Software Upgrades

Or as I like to say, "Oooooooooo! Shiny!!" Everyone wants the best, the newest, the fastest electronics. Same with software. Software is only as good as its ability to adapt, expand, and grow with you as a consumer. Sure, it was great 6 months ago, but now you have different needs, or the industry has changed. Does your software change and grow with you?

Make sure you keep BusBoss software updates turned on! When a client calls with issues or problems, or a need for better efficiency with our products, our goal is not only to try to resolve that issue, but to see where we can improve our software at every turn. Not all improvements are good for everyone. So, if a client has a request for something that is extremely specific to them, we take the time to work with them to create a custom solution, whether it be a report or automated function.

I love working for this company. What I have learned throughout my experiences – and brought into my new career – is that strong customer service is invaluable to keeping a client happy. Being able to communicate effectively is a cornerstone of customer service. That doesn't just mean talking – it means listening. Listening to the frustration, or anxiety, or panic, or even confusion that the client is experiencing. By listening for the clues to ask the right questions, it allows you to reassure that the human being on the other end of the phone is there to help.

Your support and empathy help build their confidence in you, the software, and eventually their own skills as a consumer. Some of the most valuable words/phrases to someone going through the learning curve are, "That's okay. You aren't going to break it. You were right. You did that correctly." Through support and encouragement, you can go from being lost in the weeds, to an empowered and confident user.

GETTING TECHNICAL HELP WHEN YOU NEED IT

Dana Moyer
"Never Not Ready"

"Thank you for calling Orbit Software. This is Dan speaking; how can I help you?"

If you're a customer, you probably know me as a ponderous, even-tempered voice on the other end of the telephone, but my job extends far beyond that. Between technical support, server management, data conversion, software testing, website development, and software documentation, I've had my hands in everything in one way or another.

Ever since I was young, I've always had an interest in technology. When my family got our first computer, I committed myself to learning as much as I possibly could about this machine. I became the family's "techie," the kid they would turn to for help with their computers, and later on in life, phones, and tablets.

When I left high school, I went to Reading Area Community College to study programming and web development. I later trained at Berks Career and Technology Center, earning my certifications in computer networking and server management. I then moved between several contract jobs before settling at Orbit Software. When I started here in 2017, it was both out of a desire to put my skills to work, and also a deep-seated need to help others.

Although I had only a few years of experience in tech support, it was through patience, dedication, and sheer tenacity, that I worked my way up to a respected position among Orbit's support staff. More than that, I can thank my coworkers for their endless encouragement that pushed me to where I am today.

Orbit Software is a small company, but that may be our greatest strength. The relative size of the business means everyone knows each other, personally and professionally. We know what each of us is capable of, what our tasks are, and who to turn to if we need help. I know I can reach out to Sean if I have questions about BusBoss's functionality, to George if I have questions about SQL programming, or to Sonia if I need direction. In turn, they know they can count on me for anything they might ask.

That kind of interoperability is important, not just for our organization, but any organization. Your employees' ability to depend on each other can make or break your company.

Redundancy, Succession, and Skill Overlap

Consider this: if you work for an organization for ten years, how would you go about resigning? Would you train your subordinates or immediate successor on your duties before you leave? Would you have them shadow you for a month? A year? Would you simply get up from your desk, say "See ya," and then walk out the door?

That may sound like a joke, but it's something I see all too often. A transportation supervisor will leave, and then another staff member will be placed in their position--sometimes from an entirely different department--and then be tasked with learning their job on the fly. As you can imagine, this can be disastrous.

If someone must succeed you, they must be able to carry out the same tasks that you did to a degree of competency. You cannot expect someone else to take over your position if they are not prepared to do your job.

It's important to remember how the responsibilities you hold fit into the greater whole of your company. For example, I'm tasked with training both our new customers and new staff members on using our software. I also assist with maintaining our backup server, testing software patches, and providing daily technical support.

What this means in practice is that I need to know our software inside and out. I need to understand how multiple types of software interact and push and pull data to and from the database. I need to understand the SQL Server suite well enough to manipulate this data directly. I also need a fundamental understanding of Microsoft Windows, Windows Server, Microsoft Office, and the ability to research and test software on my own.

My coworkers are no different. Each one of our support staff is trained on how to use our software in the same way, and each of us is expected to know how to support it well enough to stand on their own.

Employee redundancy is paramount. More important than hiring, perhaps more than training, is ensuring that no individual staff member is so critical to your operation that their absence brings the company to a screeching halt.

Data Normalization and Cleanup

Staring down an Excel spreadsheet may not be the most intimidating thing in the world, but maybe that depends on who you ask. One can find themselves lost in the cascade of numbers, codes, names, addresses and anecdotes. More so if the data is disorganized from the outset.

Consistency is another matter. Ensuring that multiple data sets align so that they can be used in conjunction with one another, is no small order. Checking data, against data, against more data can be time-consuming and tedious.

Data preparation is extremely important to our business. Making sure that your data is clean and cohesive from the outset ensures that it can be processed smoothly. I believe that one or two errors is nothing earth-shattering. Mistakes are to be expected; but like any ship, one too many leaks and the whole thing sinks.

So how do you get your data from "as is" to "workable?" The answer: communication, verification, and standardization. This is what we call "data normalization."

We begin by clearly communicating what data we need, and what we need it for. Typically, when a new customer comes to us, we have an introductory meeting where we brief the customer on how our software works and our data conversion process. We then provide the customer with a series of excel sheets that will need to be filled out with data for schools, students, drivers, bus routes and other information.

Once we receive the client's data, we begin checking it for common errors. These include:

- Missing student ID numbers

- Duplicate student entries

- Unlocatable addresses or bus stops (e.g., "Across from Mailbox" or "Old Church")

- Students attending schools out of district or otherwise not recognized

Data cannot be entered into the system until it has been verified by our staff. We don't want to begin processing information until we are certain it is error-free, or at least as much as is humanly possible. As George often says, "good in, good out."

At any time during this process, we will reach out to the customer with questions, comments, and status updates. If there are any issues with the data, we go to the client *first*. It's their information, after all. They know it better than anyone else.

When we are certain that our data is viable, then we can begin to move the data into standardized import templates. Once these spreadsheets have been formatted and prepared, we can then use a series of programs and utilities to process the data into a SQL database that can be read by the BusBoss client.

The three most common templates we create are:

- Student Import Sheet - containing all students' personal data

- Bus Route Sheet - containing all bus routing information

- Stop Temp Table Sheet - containing all students' bus stop assignments

After the data has been moved, then we begin reviewing the information as it appears in BusBoss. Several staff members begin verifying the customer's database against the information that was provided to us at initial contact. It is only after the database has passed inspection that we will provide it to the customer.

As you can see, every step of this process is extremely strict and very formalized. We hold our data to a high standard, and for good reason: it is the foundation of your student system.

User Tasks and Responsibilities

Once we have completed installation and training, you're free to enjoy your new software at your leisure. Your troubles are gone, and any problems will work themselves out on their own. ...Right?

It's easy to treat a new tool as a fix-all, but we all know it's never that simple. Software shouldn't make your responsibilities disappear but create new and more efficient tasks for you and your coworkers.

Ongoing Tasks

Regardless of the software you use, it's best to get into a maintenance routine. Consider what information will need to be kept up to date on a constant basis and use this knowledge to build a regular task list. In our case, one of our customers' most common tasks is updating student information. This includes:

- Adding new students to the database

- Assigning students to stops, and to bus routes

- Enrolling or withdrawing students as they attend or leave school for the year

- Updating address and contact information for students

All of these items can be accomplished either by hand or by importing student data into the database.

When not working with student information, you can commit yourself to cleaning up your data:

- Ensure that all of your students are accounted for and routed properly

- Be sure that your data is consistent between your student system, routing system, and others

- Check that your routes have no issues with navigation

- Run reports for your drivers or administrative staff

Keeping your data current and consistent gives your coworkers a reliable foundation to work from. However, not every task will need to be handled on a daily basis.

Long-term Goals

Tackling student routing may seem like a big challenge, but it may help to develop larger overarching goals rather than trying to do everything at once.

- Keep maintenance records for your buses current

- Track odometer records throughout the school year

- Track mileage for your routes, including miles with and without students

- Enter contact information for your staff members

Any number of things can happen during a school year. Students will come and go, and staff will change. What you should focus on is preparing for things you know will happen with a level of certainty:

- Perform student rollover for the new school year.

- Prepare student and transportation data for state reporting.

- Estimate expenditures so that you can budget for the upcoming year.

With these goals in mind, you will be better prepared to handle whatever the year throws at you.

State Reporting

It's no secret that operating a transportation service costs money. When you consider the cost of maintaining buses, fuel, building maintenance, and paying salaries and benefits to drivers, mechanics and dispatchers, the charges can add up very quickly. While you aren't likely to negate these costs, assistance is readily available.

Within the United States, the government offers reimbursement for transportation services performed by any publicly funded school district. For many districts, this is a great opportunity to recuperate losses from the costs of providing transportation.

In most states, you can request forms from your Department of Education or download them from their website. As you may imagine, you will fill these out, and submit them to the state, so they can release your reimbursements.

While reimbursement is handled differently from state to state, most states require that the reporting district provides a count of students on each bus and how much mileage is driven by each bus on an average day. Pennsylvania, for example, requires a Pupil Transportation Data Worksheet containing a headcount for each bus route. No to mention how many miles are driven with and without students. These counts are taken once a month from October through May in a given school year.

It's important to keep to a regular schedule when tracking your data. Record odometer readings at least once a month. Keep track of changes in your bus routes from month to month or week to week, which students are riding and how many on each bus. Determine how many miles the bus travels with students, and without. By recording this information consistently, you can help yourself get into the proper mindset to produce accurate reporting data for the state, thereby ensuring maximum reimbursement.

In addition, you must consider:

- Student Entrance dates

- Student Withdrawal dates

- Holidays

- Bus & Vehicle Usage

If you operate a transportation contracting business, you may be asked to provide information to the school districts that you work for. It is their responsibility to report this information to the state.

Chapter Recap

- Software has been installed and training has been completed, now what?

- Don't let the software just sit on the shelf!

    o Community Forum
    o Software Support
    o Software Upgrades
    o Software Training
    o Daily Tasks
    o Weekly Reviews
    o Monthly Goals
    o Yearly Clean-Up
    o Submitting State Reports

- **BusBoss Planner** - take what you've just learned and make it happen in real life?

ROUTE OPTIMIZATION
Redistricting, Tiering/Bell Times, and Stop Analysis

Sonia Mastros
"Golf Goddess"

The Problems Facing School Districts Without Route Optimization

Many districts fail to realize how much money they're losing on a daily basis from unoptimized routes, especially if they're using outdated maps or still plotting out routes by hand. Even in a small town, the number of potential routes for busses is nearly infinite. Someone creating routes by hand is rarely, if ever, going to achieve a truly optimal solution for their bus routes.

However, beyond the raw route calculations, districts with outdated maps and routing techniques are also creating other problems for themselves:

★ Maps can take months to create by hand, effectively creating an all-summer job for someone who probably could be using their time more productively. It's little wonder some schools continue using outdated routes rather than revise their maps.

★ Changes to the routing due to enrollment changes are usually made on an adhoc basis; thus, creating routes that are even less optimized.

★ The process of adding and changing routes is often complex enough that recent student transfers may not even be able to take the bus at first if the approval process is a lengthy one.

★ Bus drivers may be hit with large changes to their routes practically overnight, with administrators merely hoping they'll be able to remember and adapt when their load changes from day to day.

★ "Lost" students being left on the bus or getting off at the wrong stop can cause panic among parents, and bad publicity.

★ New roads added to the local street system may be overlooked entirely, even if they could help reduce drive times.

When times were prosperous and school budgets were higher, schools could afford to lose a bit of money on bus transportation. Now, when every penny counts, these small problems overall can add up and cause financial drains.

Optimization Review Checklist

Student Information

First and foremost, you must make sure you have up to date and complete information stored for every student. Whether you are getting this from your SIS or other type of database, the key is to have *one* system to depend on for accurate information. You should have access to not only their general information, such as student name, address, and school they attend, but other safety information and unique needs. This can include information such as emergency contacts, babysitter or split custody information, special needs requirements, and anything else that either the driver or you should know to make sure their routing needs are met. You should also have access to any student specific routing documents and even student pictures. The more information, the better. Be sure to have a system in place to keep this information updated at all times. Not only will this prove to be invaluable in case of an emergency, but it will also help with state reporting to ensure accurate counts for maximum reimbursement.

Driver Utilization

You must have a system in place to store not only general information, but availability; what days and/or nights the driver can work? Are they able to work evenings or weekends? All this must be in a central location for both your regular drivers as well as substitute drivers. In addition, you should track all required employment checks that have been completed and if they are up to date, or if they still need to be done. The system should also track attendance, testing, and violations. Lastly, do not depend on your drivers to let you know when their recertification, physical, or license will have to be renewed. Put measures in place to alert you when this is about to happen, to ensure you never have drivers on the road illegally.

Bus Utilization

Be sure to have a record of every vehicle at your disposal. Make sure to know the type, capacity, special equipment available, and inspection date. This will serve you well when optimizing your routes. For instance, you could possibly send a bigger bus to a certain area to pick up more students instead of sending two smaller buses. Understand your fleet and its capabilities so you can better utilize them. You should ask yourself the following questions:

- Do you fill your buses to capacity?
- Do you ever combine certain routes to fill up more seats on the bus?
- Is it possible to make the students ride a bit longer to achieve this?
- Do you ever combine routes to eliminate the need for an extra bus?
- Can you use different bus sizes, such as bigger buses, to fit more kids?
- Have you considered the special needs capacity of the bus?

Bus Stop Utilization

Locations and grouping of bus stops are especially important. Do you have a maximum walk to stop distance for your riders? Are you utilizing them to create optimal group stops?

The more times your bus stops, the longer it idles and the more gas it uses. If you can lessen the amount of stops by utilizing better stop placement, this could add up to a huge cost savings. You should ask yourself the following questions:

- Are you aware of any unsafe areas that are not ideal for stops?
- Is there a location in which a house stop may be safer for a child?

- How are your bus stops created?

- Are you utilizing the school's maximum walk-to-stop distances?

- Could you create more group stops as opposed to house stops?

- Could you further combine group stops?

- Have you ensured that your special needs students have been assigned to house stops requiring right side pickups?

- What are the realities of your community's road system and topography?

All of these scenarios must be considered when locating your stops.

Run optimization

This encompasses how your runs are created. You must always compare which option is the least expensive, yet still keeping your students safe. Is it by shortest time or shortest distance? What works better for your operation? This must be done while taking into account travel restrictions, such as roadblocks or hazardous roads. Are you providing your drivers accurate driving directions? Are they following them? All this must be accurate for your state reimbursement. Whatever you use to plan your routes, you must have the ability to easily update and change them. It is extremely important to make your routes as safe and efficient as possible for both the students and the district.

Zones

To have total route optimization, you must have district-wide defined zones. We suggest breaking out the attendance zones into school specific walker and rider zones. This will ensure that your walk-to-school distances are maximized so that you are only transporting eligible riders.

Sex Offender and Threat zones, such as hazardous corners, known gang or drug use areas, should be well defined to ensure student safety not only for their stop location, but also for the driver to avoid these areas.

Redistricting and Boundary Analysis

Even if your district is not in the process of a redistricting, it is always good to understand how your district boundaries impact your routing. You should constantly be looking at ways to create optimal routes. In doing so, you can analyze attendance borders as well as analyze your bell times. Do you tier your routes? If not, could you? This could potentially save thousands per year on your fuel and fleet maintenance costs. Another option is to look into instituting transfer locations for your private schools. Instead of sending out multiple buses to the same school, you could have them all ride one bus. By doing so, could they be brought into a central location to transfer? All these ideas should be looked at and mapped out in order to come up with the best possible routing solutions for your area. Once you have compiled all your findings, you can then present them as options for minimizing costs.

GPS Vehicle Tracking

If your vehicles are not equipped with a tracking device, consider investing in GPS tracking. This will help your district know if the routes you are giving your drivers are actually being followed. Estimate fuel and vehicle maintenance costs based on the actual miles traveled by each vehicle, as well as creating accurate state reports to maximize reimbursement. In addition, you can be alerted to routing deviations, reckless driving, speeding, and idling. Tracking also tells you where the vehicle is located at all times, in case of an emergency.

Student Ridership & Tracking

In addition to tracking the vehicles, you may consider tracking your students. The students can carry Mifare, NFC, or RFID enabled cards and scan them every time they get on or off the bus. This allows you to capture and store accurate ridership attendance. This will help you understand what stop locations are not being utilized, as well as allow for intentional overloading. The most important aspect to this is that you have a record of where the student got on and off the bus in case of an emergency.

Human Oversight

Last but not least, let's touch on human oversight. Everything that we have discussed so far could potentially be done manually. But it is important to have checks and balances. You should have some sort of dashboard that alerts you when information is incorrect or missing. When optimizing your routes, it's critical to have every student accounted for and data integrity is of the utmost importance. The last suggestion we have is to invest in software. Whether it's a Microsoft application like Access or Excel, or a routing and scheduling software program like BusBoss, the program must be able to handle as much as possible. We are all human and we all make mistakes, so one way to prevent them is to put all of this information into a software program that will have the checks and balances built in.

METRICS AND KPIS

George Mastros
"Master of Algorithms"

I have the best job in the world!

I take great pride in my work. I often think how school districts use BusBoss to optimize their routes in such a way that it significantly reduces their total costs. I used to think that it would ultimately allow districts to reduce the burden on their taxpayers. Now that I am older, and perhaps a bit wiser, I realize (and hope) that they use the savings realized by BusBoss to improve the education quality they provide to their students. Reducing costs can be challenging without considering the impact it will have on the students being transported.

What kinds of KPIs do you measure?

There are many things to consider when attempting to reduce costs. Probably the most important thing to realize is that the average bus can only accommodate approximately 50 students at a time. This is an abysmally small number in relation to the total number of students in the district. Unfortunately, each bus you use can incur significant costs such as driver salary, insurance, maintenance, and fuel. These costs can easily accumulate and are multiplied by the large number of buses you use. Therefore, when you consider reducing costs, the first thing you should consider is reducing the total number of buses you use.

Students Per Bus

This is probably the most important metric that you should consider. This number is relatively easy to determine. Simply stand outside the school building(s) and count the number of students getting off each bus and the total number of students each bus can accommodate. Obviously, you want to maximize the number of students per bus. There are some constants here that cannot be changed. You cannot change the number of students that attend your district, and you cannot change the number of students that each bus accommodates. You can, however, change the number of students assigned to each bus. Specifically, if your buses are not full (or nearly full) when they deliver students to their school. In this case, there is probably room for improvement, which means that you may be able to reduce the number of buses your district uses.

For example, if you currently use 50 buses, and each bus has 5 spare seats, you could reduce this to 2 spare seats per bus, which utilizes 3 extra seats per bus. If your bus capacity is 50 students per bus, and you utilize 3 more seats per bus, this would represent approximately 150 students, which is about 3 full buses. Eliminating 3 buses from your fleet means that you also eliminate 3 salaries, 3 insurance payments, and more. This adds up to significant savings simply by using 3 extra seats per bus.

I apologize for making this sound easy, because in reality it isn't that easy. Using school bus routing software can make this process easier, especially when that software has all of the features that BusBoss has.

Miles Per Bus

Sometimes it is not possible to reduce the number of buses that you use. Fortunately, this is not the end of the story. You can also realize modest savings by modifying your routes in a way that reduces the distance that each bus travels. Unfortunately, school buses are quite big and clunky, rendering them to be a bit of a fuel hog. Diesel-powered school buses average 6.1 miles per gallon, while gasoline-powered buses average 5.5 miles per gallon.

Most school buses average over 20,000 miles per year and last approximately 12 to 15 years. If you can reduce the travel distance for each route, you can reduce the wear and tear on your buses and save costs on fuel, maintenance, and maybe even insurance. Reducing distances can be painful, especially if you are not using a full featured routing and scheduling system like BusBoss.

Students Per Stop

One subtle way to improve the efficiency of your operation is to increase the number of students assigned to each stop. This can be a bit controversial because the only way to accomplish this is to make students walk further to their bus stop. This can be problematic because every student and parent would prefer to have a house stop. These are inefficient because it requires the bus to stop more often. What's worse is that it also requires the bus to travel on every road where students live. By creating group stops, you can eliminate many of the roads that the bus must travel, which reduces the time necessary to transport children to and from school. It also reduces the total travel distance, allowing you to reduce costs.

When considering group stops, you must then think about student safety. This is more important than reducing costs. It is not always safe for a child to walk to a group stop. If a child lives on a hazardous road, with a lot of fast-moving traffic, a child should have a house stop. There are a lot of complicated laws and or rules for determining whether a road is hazardous, considering factors such as: pedestrian related accidents, road width, traffic volume, railroads, sidewalks, shoulder width, sight distance, speed limit and perhaps other factors. Hazardous conditions are usually controlled by the state that the district is in, so laws and regulations may vary depending on the district.

Yearly Route Review Process

When family and friends ask me what I do, they are often surprised because school bus routing is often ignored by most people. In fact, it is the mark of a good transportation director when people don't think about transportation in general because it indicates that your buses are usually on schedule with minimal disruptions.

Unfortunately, this can lead to an ethos of "don't rock the boat", which can be dangerous because complacency leads to inefficiencies. Many transportation directors simply "tweak" routes each year to accommodate entering and departing students. This is probably the safest approach to preparing routes for the start of school because the route for most students wouldn't change by much. In doing so, the bus stop location stays the same, the bus and driver would stay the same, and the times would be similar, changing by only a few minutes.

Making significant changes to your routes can be problematic for your students, parents, and drivers because consistency is comfortable. Unfortunately, comfortable does not always mean efficient. To be clear, I'm not suggesting that bus routes should be changed every time a new student enters the district, or a child moves out of the district but, changing routes at the start of each school year is appropriate and expected.

Optimizing your routes can be time consuming but saving routes and minimizing travel distances have great benefits. This process should occur *every* year. Before beginning, it's important that you have the appropriate data necessary to ensure a realistic outcome. Specifically, when preparing routes for the next school year, you'll need to know who your new students are, what school they will be attending, and where they live. Specifically, you will have an entire grade's worth of students that are graduating and others that are either starting kindergarten and preschool. Approximately 15% of your students will be different from year to year. Additionally, you will have students that rollover from one school to another, maybe requiring that their route to school be changed.

Importing Student Information System Data

Preparing routes for the next school year requires a lot of planning and a lot of data. To accomplish this, you can sit at your keyboard with a stack of papers and an exceptionally large cup of coffee. Alternatively, you could import your student demographic data into BusBoss, which saves a lot of time and a lot of typographical errors.

Importing data is probably the single most important thing you can do to ensure a successful bus routing system. BusBoss can import data from various sources, including PowerSchool, eSchool Plus, eSchool Data, Tenex, Genesis, and various other sources. Many of these student information systems have built-in and/or custom processes for exporting data in the BusBoss format. As such, BusBoss allows for importing from data files in a more automated manner. To be clear, there are many ways to import data into BusBoss.

When importing, you need to know your data. Some school districts include all students in their student information system, and others only include public school students. When performing your imports, you need to know if the data incorporated includes *all* students or just public-school students. Private, charter and special ed. students may have to be manually entered, but they don't have to be included in the import process.

Master of Algorithms

As a software developer, I adore data. Data is the driving force behind almost every decision you make. Some data is obviously important while other bits of data are less so. For routing children to school, the most important information is where you are transporting them from and where you are transporting them to.

You need to know where they live and which school they attend. Without this, you cannot route the child. Other important information includes grade, special requirements, guardians, alternate routing addresses, etc. BusBoss captures all this information and a lot more. Each piece of data is important for various reasons. This is a short list of our top examples.

Student's Date of Birth

When routing students, the address and school the child attends are the most important bit of information needed. Date of birth is only used during the graduation process. This process does a lot of obvious things like promoting the student by one grade and assigning a new school if the previous school does not accommodate the student's new grade.

For those students with special needs, they are often the school district's responsibility until the student is 21 years old. This is usually considered on the first day of school. If a special needs child is less than 21 years old on the first day of school, the district is responsible for them for the whole year.

The date of birth is also important for preschool students. If a preschool student is 5 years old on the first day of school, they should attend Kindergarten. Otherwise, they should remain a preschool student. BusBoss calculates the age of the child and will promote the student only if the age allows for it.

Special Needs Students

Routing special needs students can be complicated and time consuming. The biggest challenge is making sure that all of the special requirements are taken care of. Some special needs students require an aide or a nurse. Some are in a wheelchair, take up more than one seat, or some even require a special type or harness. Unless you are using software, tracking this information for all your special needs students can bury you in paperwork. With software, all of the information is stored in the same place and can be instantly accessed when the need arises.

You can do all of this yourself, hire BusBoss to do this or outsource your entire transportation operations.

Chapter Recap

- How much money can you save the district while still ensuring student safety?

- Services are available to analyze your current routing to determine changes that can be made before actually making them.

    - Route Optimization
    - Redistricting
    - Tiering/School Bell Times Review
    - Stop Location Analysis

OUTSOURCING TO BUS CONTRACTORS
Pros & Cons

Sonia Mastros
"Golf Goddess"

To Outsource or Not to Outsource?

For decades, this has been a pressing question which student bus transportation coordinators have wrestled with.

A study done by The Mackinac Center for Public Policy looked at outsourcing by school districts in several states, including Pennsylvania. They found some interesting distinctions that made Pennsylvania a special case for school bus contracting:

- Pennsylvania has the highest number of districts outsourcing student bus transportation services of the states surveyed, at two-thirds.

- Pennsylvania has many choices in outsourced bus services to choose from, with dozens of different providers operating.

- Contracts with multiple private transportation companies appeared to be fairly common. One school district had contracts with *seventeen* providers.

Clearly, the wealth of options in private transportation contractors has made it an attractive proposition for many Pennsylvanian districts. But is it right for *your* district?

Forrest Tarver, Supervisor of Transportation from Upper Darby School District stated, *"When weighing all of your options you should plan to be firm with whatever decision is made and stick to the message that the best solution for your particular situation has been made. Once you outsource it may be a big struggle to bring it back inhouse."*

Looking to the Bottom Line: The Pros and Cons of Student Bus Transportation Outsourcing

There are some clear and obvious reasons as to why a school district might choose to outsource their bus and other transportation services:

- They no longer have to pay for the costs of maintaining a fleet.

- Training and development of bus drivers is likewise eliminated from the budget. Special needs training is still absorbed by the district.

- Most legal\insurance responsibility for any accidents falls on the contractor, rather than the school district.

- Districts which previously owned their own bus fleet, can usually sell those assets off for a substantial one-time cash influx, which is generally in the hundreds of thousands of dollars.

For a school district facing severe budget shortfalls, hiring independent contractors can be an excellent *quick fix* for their financial situation. The reduced costs combined with the extra money generated by selling assets can go a long way towards mitigating an unfavorable financial situation.

But does it make sense in the longer term? That's harder to say.

Services provided by district staff focused on the quality of your student's education should not be dismissed. The quality, availability, on-time performance, internal controls, IEP accountability, and local district collaboration may outweigh any cost savings found with outsourcing.

Other schools surveyed, such as Rockwood School District in Missouri, found that even the lowest bids for contracted services were costlier than their own self-operated expenses. Other districts tend to view their self-owned bus fleet as an investment; measuring its worth in terms of opportunities it presents them.

Whether outsourcing is a good value largely depends on whether a district is looking at the short-term or long-term, as well as the offers on the table.

What Options Are Available for Improving School Bus Services?

The options available to schools in this situation are regrettably few. As unfortunate as it is to say, a person creating bus routes by hand will never be able to out optimize a computer except by pure luck.

These sorts of computational problems involving millions of alternatives are exactly what computers are best at figuring out, and humans are the worst at it. A hand-created map virtually guarantees buses will be driving too long and making too many stops. It may even require more buses than are necessary.

There is a potential "Do It Yourself" solution, like making use of Google Maps or a personal GPS system to work out routes. This can help, but such systems are still not designed to deal with balancing multiple routes at once. DIY maps created with existing free map programs still won't be as well designed as those created by a system that natively can handle dozens of routes simultaneously.

Outsourcing is another option; many school districts have been outsourcing their routing since the 1990s. While this initially provided cost savings to many districts, as time has gone on, those savings are drying up.

While a full look into the causes of this trend is beyond the scope of this book, the short version is that once a school has sold off its bus fleet, it's not going to have the money to purchase a new one. The contractors know this, and the result is the ongoing cost hikes to a captive market that quickly erase the initial savings.

Finally, there are outsourced contractors who offer route optimization services specifically, but this is a solution that offers few true benefits to a school district. It adds an extra layer of bureaucracy to a sector arguably already choked with paperwork and in doing so, creates a system where the district has to call in the consultant whenever they want to change their routes. Like with outsourced buses, this only leads to increased costs and inefficiency as time goes on.

When to Know When Your District Needs to Outsource Student Transportation

There are certainly pros and cons to outsourcing student transportation, and many administrators hold strong opinions on the matter. With more and more districts facing the stark reality of decreased budgets, transportation outsourcing is becoming a common practice.

Why Outsource Your Transportation Services?

Cost is one of the main reasons that school districts choose to outsource their transportation services. Outsourcing saves school districts from paying not only operation and maintenance costs, but also personnel costs. Those who are for outsourcing point out that money saved by contracting out bus services, can then be funneled back into the educational system.

A case could be made that outsourcing also saves and increases safety and efficiency by providing drivers with access to training, equipment, and advanced technology that might not be available at the district level. Proponents also suggest that outsourcing reduces district liability.

The Challenges of Outsourcing

Outsourcing can also be met with objections from district officials and the community at large. Arguments often include loss of jobs and loss of control.

Outsourcing does not always equal a balanced budget. Carefully weighing the costs, along with the pros and cons, is vital to making the right decision for your district. One concern to consider is whether your district will have the capital to re-invest in a new bus fleet if outsourcing does not work out.

If your district is making the difficult decision of whether or not to outsource transportation services, it's important to keep in mind that there are tools which are available at a reasonable cost that can dramatically increase efficiency.

For example, school bus routing software offers tools that help districts better manage their buses, which in turn optimize routes for efficiency. A hybrid solution can also be used, where the district creates the routes then puts them out to bid for contractors to run. This way the district can retain control to ensure student safety and maximize cost savings.

Investing in management software can also save big bucks for even smaller districts to operate their fleet with or without the help from a large transportation outsourcing company.

Seeking advice from industry experts will help you make the best decision for your school district. An industry professional can help you determine if technology can help improve the efficiency of your transportation system. In some cases, even providing you with additional options.

Choosing whether or not to outsource student transportation is a tough decision, but it can work out well. Either way, weigh the pros and cons and consider all of your options to find the best solution for your school district.

The Challenge for Both Options: Overcoming the School Bus Driver Shortage

Districts that want to keep their buses moving on-time and on-schedule will need to be creative and dedicated to ensuring the necessary staffing of their bus routes. This section has been written specifically to help school districts and bus contractors achieve these goals. In it, we will take a deeper look at the problems surrounding bus driver recruitment and retention, while suggesting hard actionable ideas for improving your own driver staffing. In addition, we will also look at recent technological advances which have been shown to significantly improve driver experience, reduce fleet costs, and enhance student safety.

School districts and bus contractors in the 21st century are facing many challenges, but one of the fastest-growing problems in modern school administration is the matter of having enough bus drivers on staff. There is a very real school bus driver shortage facing the nation, and it is only getting worse as time goes on.

School Bus Fleet Magazine has conducted multiple surveys across the country over the years, tracking the state of school's fleets. In 2010, seventy-one percent of districts said they had a lack of drivers. By 2015, that statistic had grown to ninety-two percent, with roughly one-fourth of respondents describing their situation as either "severe" or "desperate." The numbers were similar for private bus contractors. ninety-four percent reported a driver shortage, with thirty percent of those describing it as "severe" or "desperate."

Why is there so much trouble with driver recruitment? Many possible factors have been suggested, including:

- Low pay/benefits

- Too much paperwork or other regulatory requirements

- Difficult working conditions

- Lack of on-the-road support or assistance options

- Too little support from management on disciplinary issues

- Outdated or antiquated buses and other equipment

- Too many conflicts with parents

- Inaccurate or outdated routing reports

The problems this shortage is causing for school districts is obvious and - statistically speaking - probably already affecting you. Many schools are being forced to "double-up" their routes; sending buses out in two waves until all students can be transported. This, however, often forces schools to delay the start of classes. It also creates disciplinary problems, particularly among students forced to wait an hour or more after the end of school.

Other districts are being forced to increase bus fees, or even cut services to some areas entirely. Both of these measures can severely disadvantage lower-income families, or potentially even create situations where children are unable to attend school.

To begin with, we will start by turning the issue around: Looking at school bus driving from the perspective of potential drivers and understanding why so many are reluctant to sign up.

Understanding What Drivers Are Looking For

It's easy to focus on one's own problems in hiring, but in a situation where demand for labor is greatly exceeding the labor supply, it's a good idea to take a broader view of it all. Why is it that good bus drivers are becoming so hard to find?

Obviously, some factors here are unavoidable. Bus drivers must possess a commercial driver's license (CDL), as well as being able to pass extensive background checks along with other factors such as drug tests. While many areas provide CDL training and licensing assistance as part of school bus driver recruitment, not all drivers qualify. These issues alone will limit the pool of available drivers and they cannot be changed - nor would anyone want to!

However, there are other factors - specific to the drivers themselves and their perception of school bus driving work - which are further limiting the labor supply. Let's take a look at some of those.

Unusual Hours

School bus driving requires a very unusual schedule for its workforce. They may only be on the clock for three or four hours per day, and they're doing so at extremely inconvenient times. A bus driver running a morning route will probably be waking up at 5 a.m., then driving for a couple hours, and then have to be back for the afternoon drive around 2 p.m. Then they will be going to bed extremely early, probably around 9-10 p.m., to be well-rested for the next morning's run.

The problem is this: Hours like that are purely part-time in terms of work, and also make it extremely difficult to hold down additional employment. This greatly limits those who are in a position to take such a job.

Relatively Low Pay and Benefits

Estimates for average bus driver wages can vary wildly, undoubtedly due to the wide disparity in districts' ability to pay. However, a number around $15 per hour seems reasonable, based on numbers from the Bureau of Labor Statistics and other sources.

While not excessively low, this is not enough for many drivers to make a living on, particularly given the difficulty they would have supplementing their income with another job. Additionally, few, if any drivers, would qualify for health, dental, or other benefits that come with a full-time job unless they were employed by the district in another capacity as well.

The Stress of the Job

It is no understatement to say that bus drivers are responsible for carrying the most precious cargo in the world. No traditional truck driver would feel as much stress over a load of produce, or even sports cars, then they would ever be being responsible for the lives of dozens of children. There is a genuine psychological toll which has to be considered.

Plus, of course, should they ever be involved in an accident, the liability issues would be personally ruinous.

On top of the "big picture" stresses, there are day-to-day stresses as well, particularly in dealing with disciplinary issues and parents. It's all too common for bus drivers to find themselves in conflicts with parents over their children's behavior. Worse, many school districts are so concerned about lawsuits that they will almost always side with the parent, leaving the bus driver with very few allies.

A Lack of Tools to Improve the Job

Many districts are still using the same pen-and-paper record keeping methods that they have used for decades. Drivers have to hand-document everything about their run from fuel use to disciplinary reports, while also having to keep track of all their passengers manually.

This can add significantly to the time burdens of the job, as well as making it unpleasant to deal with.

There Are Better Options on The Table

Simply put, there is often truly little compelling reason for a person to go into bus driving when it can be such a stressful job that also makes it difficult to earn a livable wage. Further, if someone were interested in taking a job that requires obtaining a commercial driver's license, there are other alternatives - such as truck driving - where CDL training is also frequently part of the recruitment package. From the perspective of a potential driver, there is often little reason to recommend school bus driving over other forms of commercial vehicle operation.

This is what modern school districts are up against. To be able to recruit bus drivers, they need to be able to provide compelling reasons for why someone would want to sign up. Smart utilization of recruitment is also necessary in finding good candidates who can meet these criteria.

Utilizing Effective Recruitment Outlets and Techniques

To hire great bus drivers, you need to find great bus driver applicants. As we discussed in the last chapter, that can be difficult given the many perceived problems one can see with school bus driving. This means that school districts who want to recruit top candidates are going to need to be creative and be willing to explore a variety of outlets for finding those candidates.

There is no "magic bullet" solution here and all the common recruitment types have their strengths and weaknesses. First, we'll look at some of those.

Examining Common Bus Driver Recruitment Methods

Online Ads

Online advertisements placed on major employment sites like Monster, CareerBuilder, and Indeed.com, are one of the most common methods of school bus driver recruitment. Most of these sites are either free or extremely inexpensive to use. The major benefit is that these services are inexpensive to utilize, and ads can run indefinitely. The big problem is that if your advertisement is too successful, you could end up with a lot of low-quality applicants which need to be manually screened out.

Job Fairs

Job fairs are excellent for face-to-face meetings and, in the right circumstances, can help discover a number of high-quality applicants. The main issue is that they are significantly more expensive to arrange than other outreach forms, including the costs of on-site staff.

Radio Ads

In most markets, radio is hurting for advertising money and will usually be able to offer incredibly good airtime rates. Air the ads at the same times of day your bus routes run. If someone's sitting around listening to the radio, there's a good chance that they could be a potential candidate. Plus, you can pre-screen listeners based on the market the radio station targets. The downside is that, like online ads, you'll likely get a large number of junk responses.

Outdoor Ads

Billboards are expensive, but ads on places like park benches usually aren't. Also, don't forget that your own school bus could be a rolling ad. Use the side of the bus to encourage interested drivers to contact the district directly.

Social Media

Social media sites like Facebook and LinkedIn are increasingly used for bus driver discovery. If your school district is already well-networked, this can be a surprisingly effective recruitment technique since many parents may know good candidates. Or in some cases, parents may even be interested in the position. However, this is also an untargeted and scattershot approach which may or may not bring results. Look to target the posts, such as posting to LinkedIn groups specifically for commercial drivers. Plus, social media is absolutely free, which makes it a great option for budget-conscious districts.

Other Free Sources

Beyond social media, there are many other free outlets online for promotional efforts school districts can take advantage of. Their own website is always a good choice, particularly if it seems likely that parents in the district might be interested in becoming drivers. Colleges and technology training centers may have students looking for part-time jobs that are available between classes. Also, look to state and local industry groups such as your state Association of Pupil Transportation or Association of School Business Officials.

Other Important Factors in Recruitment

No matter what form of outreach you deploy, get creative with your messaging. Be aware of the objections mentioned and look for a more positive spin which could make the position seem more attractive. For example, one set of creative ads we've seen on the sides of buses used messages like, "As long as kids get evenings and weekends off, so will you!" and "You'll never take your work home with you. In fact, it's illegal."

That sort of positive spinning will go a long way, particularly when pitched as an alternative to more traditional nine to five jobs.

Likewise, when interviewing bus drivers face-to-face, be reassuring and try to emphasize the highlights of the job. Make sure to note any and all benefits that accompany the job, such as CDL training. Be prepared for them to raise some objections like the ones we've discussed and have responses ready. In fact, it could potentially be a red flag if they have no objections at all.

Finally, never neglect to have extensive background checks. No matter how badly a school district needs drivers, they should never use that as an excuse to skimp on due diligence. The risks are simply too high.

So, once you've recruited your school bus drivers, how do you hang onto them? Let's examine best practices for bus driver retention.

Keeping Your Drivers Happy

It's one thing to successfully recruit school bus drivers, but it's another thing to then hang onto them. For years, bus driving has seen higher-than-normal turnover rates, a problem which only contributes to the overall issue of driver shortages.

Annual turnover varies greatly from district to district, but rates anywhere from ten percent to over twenty percent have been reported in recent years.

For schools which already have too few bus drivers, even one or two drivers quitting can cause significant hardships for the entire district. In many cases, there is simply no safety net. There have even been reports of schools having to cancel classes due to drivers quitting.

So, it's no exaggeration to say that one of the primary concerns of a transportation coordinator should be the retention of existing drivers.

Tips for Improving Driver Retention

Wages and Benefits

- Compare your pay rates to nearby districts. Pay raises are difficult to budget, but it may be necessary if you aren't competitive.

- Consider offering medical and or dental benefits to drivers with a few years of loyalty and experience.

- Allow investment into retirement programs.

- Offer drivers other employment opportunities in the district, particularly during non-driving hours and over the summer, even if these roles aren't driving-related.

- Be willing to offer premiums for summer driving.

- Offer equalized 12-month pay schedules, like teachers can receive, to compensate for the potential lack of summer employment.

- Make it possible for substitute drivers to be promoted to full-time driver status if need arises.

- Remember the "give 'em the pickle" principle, which can also apply to employee morale. If a driver makes a request which would be cheap or easy to fulfill, it's usually better to let them have it than to risk them becoming disgruntled over a minor matter.

Rewards and Recognition

As a rule, bus drivers tend to feel unappreciated.

Almost any rewards and recognition will improve morale.

- Make branded attire such as logo shirts, hats, or jackets free or inexpensive. They also make good prizes.

- Offer driver referral bonuses, either in cash or merchandise.

- Offer job-related perks such as preferential parking as rewards for good performance.

- Give occasional free dinners for drivers such as BBQ or pizza.

- Consider giving awards for things like safety records and gas usage.

- Have clever names for your awards like "Going the Distance" or "Spotlight on Success" to make them seem more special.

- Post the awards somewhere prominent for everyone to see. Include the driver's photo to make it even more personal.

Information and Awareness

- Do community outreach. Encourage the public - particularly parents - to be appreciative of their school bus drivers.

- Promote your department within the school district. In doing this, you might even find more interested drivers that way.

- Set up student programs to encourage and educate proper bus safety.

- Create safety videos to play during special events, assemblies, parent-teacher night, etc.

- Contact City Hall and the Mayor's office to see if they'd be interested in doing an officially sponsored school bus recognition or safety program for the community.

- Participate in a community parade by having your best drivers ride in or stand next to a nice clean bus. Do not use your newest bus since it may give the impression the district has too much money since it can afford a new bus.

Community Building

- In general, don't make your drivers feel like they're "out of the loop" or not "real" district employees. Include them in anything other district employees are involved in.

- Be willing to stick up for your drivers in disputes with parents when the driver's actions were reasonable. Driver morale will plummet if they're expected to maintain discipline with unruly children, and yet are always overruled (or even disciplined) if the parent complains.

- Assign or elect driver representatives for local organizations such as the Chamber of Commerce or Rotary Club.

- Encourage drivers to connect with each other and other district employees based on shared hobbies or interests. Have a bulletin board (online or offline) for setting up groups based around hobbies.

- Take some personal interest in your drivers. Send out birthday cards. Have informal chat-lunches with them.

- Set up official avenues of communication so that drivers always feel they have the ability to talk to those higher-ups.

- Always be on time when setting meetings with drivers. Their job is intensely time-focused, and in the long-run, they'll appreciate the reciprocation.

- If the drivers have a common room, do something to spruce it up every year, even if it's something simple like new chairs or new paint.

- Create a Transportation Advisory Council which is intended to let drivers bring concerns or complaints to higher administration in a structured fashion.

- Be sure drivers have access to district resources like computer labs.

- Don't forget retirees! They could still be called upon for occasional substitution or field trip work. Send them birthday cards to stay in touch.

Ongoing Education and Development

- Look to implement systems that allow you to monitor driver performance such as reducing fuel consumption.

- Offer coaching opportunities.

- Offer paid training, or else reimburse training costs from reputable trade schools, colleges, or universities.

- For any mandatory training sessions, look to optimize them and reduce the time drivers have to spend in classrooms. Consider learn-at-your-own-pace online learning systems.

- Create cross-training opportunities for non-drivers who may be interested in driving but can only train for it in their spare time.

- Have periodic ride-a longs from administrators which are intended to be educational and not judgmental. Learn what drivers are dealing with to help train them in practical ways of handling situations.

- Consider adding technological solutions that can reduce driver burdens such as student-monitoring systems.

- If adding technology, be sure to always have someone available to train drivers on their use. Some may not be overly familiar with computers and similar systems.

Above All: Listen to your Drivers

No matter what else you do to incentivize your drivers and by keeping them happy, be sure to always listen to their ideas and suggestions. Their time spent on the road and dealing with their routes on a day-to-day basis, are going to give them insights worth considering. Plus, it will make them feel welcome, thus keeping keep their morale high.

Finally, when a driver does leave the district, always try to conduct an exit interview to find out why and incorporate that into your future planning. In short, the better you treat your drivers, the more likely they are to remain with the district in years to come. Having a group of happy drivers creates real security within the transportation system, which can pay off throughout the year in both tangible and intangible ways.

Next, we'll be looking at how improvements in technology can help you optimize your fleet while improving safety with solid long-term returns on the investment.

Technological Solutions for Improving Drivers' Experiences

Finally, let's talk about modern technology. School buses have not changed very much over the years. There are new technologies available which can significantly enhance your bus drivers' experience. In doing so, it would bring significant savings to your district as well! In many cases, investment in these technologies can turn into a true win-win-win scenario. They can keep students safer, make your drivers happier, and reduce your own overall operating costs. There are two main types of technology going into school buses today, which can either be used together or separately: GPS navigation systems and RFID-based student tracking.

Major Technologies Which Improve Your Transportation System and Bus Driver Experience

GPS Devices in Buses Make Sense

We see that GPS navigation systems are standard in many kinds of vehicles, yet their usage in school buses is lagging behind - probably due to upgrade expenses. This is unfortunate because they almost inevitably pay for themselves, and often in a noticeably short amount of time. When combined with software in the administration office, the benefits are numerous:

- Never lose track of your buses. Ever.

- Should a bus ever deviate from its planned course or stop by the side of the road, for example a flat tire, you're notified quickly.

- Drivers facing obstacles, such as thick rush-hour traffic or unexpected construction, can calculate and follow new routes.

- Onboarding new drivers is expedited since the GPS Navigation System can guide them through their route without memorization.

- Monitor your drivers' safety performance. Are they really coming to a full stop at train tracks? You'll know every time.

- Monitor bus performance such as gas mileage. This can often alert you of minor maintenance issues with the bus early on before they become costlier breakdowns.

- Calls from parents asking where their child is, can be answered more quickly and with greater precision when you can track every bus.

Additionally, the software can collect on-the-road data, which is where you can really start optimizing, particularly if you feed your bus's own maintenance data into the system. You can compare routes not just in terms of time, but also in terms of matters like fuel costs or tire wear. You can even use the data to recalculate your bus routes - potentially cutting entire routes without sacrificing any stops.

Onboard Cameras Protect Everyone

Another highly popular system to install on buses is video surveillance cameras. Depending on the setup, they can either record locally or - when connected to a sufficient mobile Internet connection - can beam their feeds directly back to the office.

The benefits here are obvious, particularly when it comes to disciplinary issues or conflicts with parents. You have video records of everything happening on the bus. So, in the scheme of things, there's simply no doubt as to whether a child did or did not do something. They can also be good for coaching bus drivers, as the video will almost always catch events that the bus driver overlooked.

Or, for live-feed cameras, the bus driver could even radio back to base and ask for help with a situation, and you'll be able to see exactly what's happening.

Onboard Tablet Systems Have Many Uses

We're beginning to see tablet computers all over the place, and fleet vehicles are no exception. Depending on the software loaded, tablets can serve a wide variety of auxiliary functions, which take a lot of stress off the driver.

Providing navigational data is one of the most popular uses when paired with a GPS system, particularly since they provide better visibility than many of the smaller handheld GPS units. Other, more specialized software systems can function as electronic logbooks - tracking maintenance, gas mileage, ridership, and more. Advanced systems can even tie directly into the bus's engine computer, collecting diagnostic data or sending information on performance problems straight to the office.

All these functions make buses safer on the road, while reducing the number of things a driver has to manually manage. Allowing them to focus as much of their attention as possible on driving should always be a priority when installing new technology.

Electronic Logging Devices Are an Inexpensive Way to Track Drivers

In an increasing number of areas around the country, it's becoming mandatory to electronically log the identity and road-hours of all large vehicle drivers. That's exactly what Electronic Logging Devices

(ELDs) do. In many cases, these devices can also handle telemetry and maintenance-tracking as well.

They aren't as robust or full-featured as some other options - such as full tablet navigation and telemetry systems - but can be an affordable option for districts who want to improve their driver tracking and reporting.

Electronic Inspection Devices Speed Checkups and Improve Maintenance

Another aspect of bus driving, which can be burdensome for both drivers and maintenance crews, is the need for frequent and thorough inspections of the buses. Electronic Inspection Devices (EIDs) can address this problem.

They work alongside RFID tags, which are embedded within the school bus; each RFID tag is attached to a "zone" which should be inspected.

Your drivers, and or maintenance crew, simply move along the bus with their EID in hand, making notes on the condition of all-important elements in each zone. These are logged electronically with timestamps.

EIDs make pre- and post-route inspections far more thorough and can often speed up the process by automating as much of it as possible. Additionally, they can allow for a huge range of reports and maintenance problems alerts - far more than a typical clipboard can hold.

There's far less chance of a maintenance issue going overlooked or unaddressed, and your reporting of issues will be much more accurate.

RFID Student Tracking Brings Peace of Mind

RFID-based tracking chips in student IDs remain a controversial idea in some places, but they're slowly coming to be accepted. The huge safety benefits outweigh minor privacy trade-offs.

This is particularly true considering that the RFID systems can't track students anywhere outside your campus and buses. Students on-campus really don't have any reason to think their movements should be private.

When it comes to school buses, the big advantage is that you will always know which students are on and off your buses. When they're tracked entering and leaving the bus, you always have a solid record of ridership. This can help with attendance tracking and improve your state funding, thanks to more-accurate reporting with hard data behind it.

Plus, you can even notify their teachers in advance that they won't be attending.

Parent/Staff Mobile Apps Share the Information

Finally, don't forget about the other people in your district with a need to keep track of your buses and their schedules! There are a number of app-based systems a school district can subscribe to which allow parents, faculty, and other authorized personnel to look up the status of buses on their routes.

They simply tie into your existing GPS or similar systems, while restricting the information provided to what that particular person needs to know (i.e., if a parent has children on Bus 3, they only see the status of Bus 3).

Besides giving parents real peace of mind, this can vastly reduce calls to your office inquiring about the status of school buses. With location information and frequently updated ETAs, parents can check for themselves to find out where their bus riding children are.

How These Systems Improve Bus Driver Experiences

Beyond improving student safety and opening up huge new opportunities to optimize your own transportation systems, a combination of technological upgrades will do a lot to make your district attractive to drivers. They can be a legitimate selling point during recruitment!

- Onboard maps and directions make navigation far easier.

- Field trips and other drives to unfamiliar locations are less stressful with computer-assisted navigation.

- Drivers with good safety or legal records can be recognized and rewarded for their skills.

- Drivers have more means of communication with the office and more avenues for getting help in unusual circumstances.

- Video cameras are an excellent way of ensuring drivers that they have sufficient protection in disputes with parents over disciplinary issues.

- Reliable electronic tracking of students takes one more burden off drivers. They aren't solely responsible for tracking ridership.

- Better tracking of maintenance issues, both in the garage and on the road, help them feel more secure about the machinery they're handling.

- Digital records-keeping is almost always easier and faster than doing them on paper.

- In general, electronic tracking or video presents facts whenever a "he said/she said" situation develops on a bus, such as over whether a student rode or if a driver is properly following the law.

Drivers know that districts who are willing to invest in their fleet for the sake of safety and efficiency, are likely to take their drivers more seriously as well. On top of all the real-world and day-to-day improvements these systems bring, that by itself can convince a driver you're worth working for.

Full Bus Staffing Is Truly Obtainable

Even though there is an industry-wide problem finding enough school bus drivers, that doesn't mean your district has to suffer. All too often, problems that districts have in recruiting and keeping drivers have to do with their own unwillingness to recognize their drivers' contributions and reward them appropriately.

A combination of effective outreach, driver-friendly policies, higher pay (if possible), and technological improvements to your buses can easily make your district one of the most attractive to bus drivers around the state. Getting the best drivers definitely requires proactive work and cooperation from administration, but it is an eminently achievable goal.

BusBoss wants to help you on your journey towards optimal bus staffing! Optimizing your routes can and will make driving easier for your drivers. If you want to find out more about how modern technology can significantly improve your transportation systems across the board, simply visit BusBoss.com for more information.

Chapter Recap

- Managing transportation in-house is one thing but should it be?

- Evaluate everything involved to determine the best option

- Vehicle Purchases

- Vehicle Maintenance

- Driver Salaries & Benefits

- Recruiting & Keeping Drivers

- Department Overhead

- Public vs. SPED Routing

- Apples to Apples Cost & Benefit Comparison

- Talk to other districts that have gone from in-house to outsourcing this process before making a final decision

- School Bus Routing Consulting Services are also a cost-effective option.

SCHOOL BUS ROUTING CONSULTING SERVICES
Transportation & Operations Management

Sonia Mastros
"Golf Goddess"

Improve the Efficiency of Your Transportation System with Route Optimization Services

School districts nationwide are facing difficult planning challenges arising from an increasing student population, an aging school infrastructure, and the increasing complexity in student reassignments and school redistricting. These challenges are shared by the communities that must fund building and renovation projects.

OSI's *School Bus Routing Consulting Services* can incorporate enrollment forecasting, land use studies, residential growth forecasts, optimal school building locations, optimally balanced attendance zones, "what-if" attendance, and walker and rider zones to provide school districts with optimized school capacity planning and routing solutions. Route Optimization services can be provided to minimize the number of buses used for routing students to and from their primary addresses.

Using proven mathematical techniques and our BusBoss routing software, OSI assists school districts dealing with difficult school redistricting plans and school planning challenges that are often conducted in a poorly articulated environment. By approaching projects quantitatively as well as qualitatively, OSI can provide school planning solutions that are driven by data and supported by policies.

OSI's *School Bus Routing Consulting Services* provide a variety of options to produce solutions for school districts experiencing issues related to growth and imbalance. Projects are tailored for an individual school district's needs, while gaining community support with school planning solutions driven by policy and supported by data.

Analyze and Improve Your Routing Inefficiencies

The bus route optimization component of the *School Bus Routing Consulting Services* is the process of creating hypothetical bus routes using your student stop locations, school assignments, bell times, maximum bus loads, and student ride times for increasing route efficiencies while reducing costs.

Optimized bus routes are generated by taking into account bus capacities, students per seat, maximum travel times, travel restrictions (height, weight and turn restrictions), road hazards (one-sided pickups), roadblocks, and one-way roads. Individual routes may also be analyzed to make manual adjustments as needed.

This service provides optimal routes, for individual schools or combined schools, by using selected criteria. These routes may then be analyzed by comparing your current route costs versus the optimized route costs.

The routes can be analyzed using complete bus schedules, passenger lists, and route driving instructions. Multiple optimized route sets may be provided to determine the best groupings or tiers and overload allowances based on specific grades.

Parent, student, and/or staff notifications will be provided showing each student's route assignment information for pick-ups and drop-offs (bus number, stop location, and time etc.) Ideally, the end goal is to reduce the number of buses and drivers needed to run your routes.

Analyze Stop Locations

Stop Locations will be analyzed to determine optimal stop locations for all of your students, based on current enrollment, road restrictions, boundaries, rider eligibility, and walk-to-stop distances set for each school.

Evaluate Walker and Rider Zones

"What-if" zones allow a school district to address specific assignment issues and refine proposals to develop a final attendance area plan.

While the optimal attendance scenarios may satisfy school board policy, there are always realities that must be considered that often cannot be formulated in the optimization model. OSI has developed tools that enable school districts to explore "what-if" walker and rider zones that address specific student reassignment issues.

In most cases, relatively few scenarios survive as potential school redistricting plans after rigorous testing of optimization constraints. Understanding that student reassignments impact communities, bus routing patterns, roadway connectivity, and other factors that cannot be included in the model, OSI utilizes a scenario builder tool so school districts can simulate "what-if", refining the attendance area scenarios.

Once the optimal attendances are generated with constraints given to OSI, the scenario builder tool allows a school district's redistricting study committee to evaluate the pros and cons of each proposal by using "what-if" scenarios. After the committee has exhausted all options using the scenario builder tool, a final plan is proposed and voted on by the school board.

Transportation Operations Committee members can be made up of district staff, such as dispatchers, routers, and also contractor staff such as managers, bus drivers and union leaders.

Recurring Route Management Services

OSI Staff can be responsible for ensuring all public-school student information is synchronized with the district's student information system. Non-public, special education, and tech school students will be compared with lists provided by administrators of each department managing these students.

Maintenance of bus routes and stop locations will be kept up to date throughout the year to account for new students. In turn, we will also update student address changes and student withdrawals.

Chapter Recap

- How much money can you save the district while still ensuring student safety?

- Services are available to analyze your current routing to determine changes that can be made before actually making them.

  - Route Optimization
  - Redistricting
  - Tiering/School Bell Times Review
  - Stop Location Analysis

- You can do all of this yourself, or you can hire BusBoss to do this for you!

BUSBOSS ROUTING, SCHEDULING & GPS TRACKING

Check out how software can make school bus routing easier

Sonia Mastros
"Golf Goddess"

ROUTING BEYOND HOME TO SCHOOL

COVID-19 Cohort Routing

Something new that came from the pandemic of 2020 has been Cohort Routing. What is Cohort Routing you ask? Well, many districts did this in an effort to keep a sense of normalcy, while still complying with social distancing.

They divided their students into groups – how many depended on the size of the school – and then scheduled them on alternate days of the week, or alternate AM/PM sessions, or alternate weeks. In some cases, a combination of any of those things. This allowed students to still have in school classes with only half of the students in the classes at a time.

We help schools achieve this by using Exception Fields, the Homeroom Field, and assigning only specific days of the week to routes using the Assign Days tab in each of the student's record.

Routing reports are then provided to drivers listing only the students scheduled for routing for each individual day of the week, AM and PM.

Second School Shuttles

Today's students have many options for learning, some which take them to different locations. Some students take classes at a vo-tech school, perhaps advanced placement classes at the local community college, or even possibly to another school in the district. These are not like regular routes because they normally run in the middle of the day to accommodate half day programs.

But is it complicated? Of course not! These shuttles are created the same way that a regular pickup and drop off route is created; it just starts and ends at the schools. How you assign your students to those routes is by selecting the appropriate routes in the student record.

Non-Pub Transfer Routes

Sometimes a bus route does not go as far as you need it to go, and a student will have to take two or more busses to get to home or school. So, what do you do when the student has to ride more than one bus to get to school? You utilize transfers. When a student needs a transfer route, the Transfer tab in the Maintain Student screen is red, and from there you can choose a route to complete the journey to their destination. Just remember: the transfer stop needs to be before the final stop for the student, or they will not be routed properly.

Transfer routes will be automatically assigned to students if there is only one transfer route available in BusBoss that goes to their final destination.

Split Custody Routing

Today's families have all sorts of dynamics, one of which is children being raised in split custody homes. Since these situations can be fluid and ever-changing without much notice, BusBoss came up with a simple way to help keep track of this sometimes overly complicated situation.

Split Custody routing is handled very much like regular routing. This will allow your student to be on both routes, going to their regular and split custody stops on any day of the week. Not to mention pick-up and drop-off. This tool will help resolve any issues that may arise.

Alternate Routes

Have you ever had a situation where you realized you should have had a backup plan? Or that scenario that had a five percent chance of happening, happened? Yeah, we've all been there. And that's one of the reasons for creating Alternate Routes.

You can create a route for when you have a snow day and need to detour around some roads that become impassable. Or perhaps the after-school programs' attendance changes throughout the year, so your routing is different. If your schools have different calendars, that may call for different routing on late arrival and/or early dismissal days.

Alternate Routes are the routes you can hold in your back pocket for the 'just in case' or 'when this happens' situations, as well as most other non-traditional routing scenarios (like field trips or sporting events). It is an excellent proactive tool for anticipating your temporary routing changes or future routing needs.

As a transportation director for school districts, there are a lot of headaches that go along with the job. Every single year, bus routes have to be created and optimized to pick up and drop off children on the right side of the street. They also have to consider the safest and shortest route possible, traffic at different times of the day and avoid streets and intersections that are not possible for buses to navigate. Parents are waiting for their children to get on and off the bus in the morning, and sometimes in extreme weather; also adding the pressure of their own schedules. So, it is imperative that the buses be on time. And if they're not, the parents want to know where their children are. Then there are sensitive issues like family disputes and custody battles that require the child to be dropped off at different places and to the right person. When everything involved in school pick-up coordinates correctly, people are generally unappreciative. But when something goes wrong, the consequences can be extreme and endanger the child.

How can school districts continue to meet the needs of their students, even as budgets continue to drop around the country?

Virtually anyone who has spent any time in US schools lately knows that this is probably the most pressing question in front of administrators. Even parents have noticed, with a recent USA Today poll noting that a lack of financial support is now the number one worry among parents with children in schools.

Reactions among school districts have been increasingly extreme as well; with more districts having to discuss radical actions such as cutting back classes to four days a week. Massive cuts to budgets are also common, with some schools looking at eliminating all non-special ed bus service entirely, despite the potential impact on students.

It's especially unfortunate when so many schools are looking at cutting their buses even though there's an inexpensive and highly effective fix available that can help virtually any struggling school.

That, in this case, is route optimization software. Rather than cutting bus budgets dramatically from the top down, route optimization allows cost cutting through better use of routing software. One software investment can preserve a school's existing bus system while helping the district provide better services to the community.

In House Route Optimization Software Brings the Greatest Savings

It's not an overstatement to say that the cost savings associated with bus route optimization can be dramatic. Depending on how poorly optimized the original bus plans were, a district can look at cutting fifty percent or more of their transportation budget without decreasing service quality.

In one case, a consulting firm found that their district could save over $300 per student per day through simple inhouse optimization strategies. Optimization software also allows ongoing operations to be conducted more quickly and efficiently. When the software is tied to the student enrollment database, the district gets an overview at a glance of every student and the route they take. New students can be added onto routes within minutes with new maps and routing delivered to the drivers accordingly. A logistical nightmare can be reduced to a single Windows application that virtually any staff member can operate and update as needed, with no extra expertise required.

Essential Ways to Schedule Safe School Bus Routes

While a few one-off states have instituted statewide policies for school bus routing, most of these decisions are made at the local school district level.

If your school is not one of the few that benefits from state government policies, it's likely you're spending a lot of time planning school bus routes. While you are tasked with balancing what is ideal for your students' safety, and with the reality of time and money, school bus routing tends to get rather complicated.

While your primary goal is establishing the safety of pick-up and drop-off locations, you must also consider how to create more efficiency in terms of your school's budgetary limitations.

Avoid "Danger Zones"

Danger zones exist in the form of traffic patterns. Determine where to load and unload students based on the location of streets with lower traffic volume. Be sure to avoid multi-lane roads where pedestrians are at most risk of injury.

Achieve Unified Communication with Your Bus Drivers

No route is a static and one-dimensional line from point A to point B. There are many factors that affect the safety and efficiency of your bus routes. For example, from planned roadwork to weather-related incidents.

Whether it's upcoming construction that completely shuts down a route or a fallen tree blocking a road after a bad storm, your drivers need the most up-to-date information to keep students safe.

Manage Rerouting Around Travel Restrictions

Awareness and management of active travel restrictions is central to effectively maintaining safe school bus routes. Manual management of the following can be challenging:

- Routing around roadblocks
- Ensuring right side pickups on hazardous roads
- Turn restrictions based on bus size
- Road restrictions based on bus height and weight
- Speed limits based on time of day
- Discovering every known area of traffic congestion
- Avoiding multi-lane roads and divided highways

With the technology of school bus routing software, your drivers can receive alerts in real-time and your maps are always updated with new roads and developments. With accurate updates, you're able to re-route buses quickly and effectively onto safer roads that get students home safely.

Make Sure Maps Are Accurately Updated

Inefficiencies abound when your maps are not accurately updated, which compromises student safety and inaccurate mileages. You need the ability to easily modify your service area maps so that your transportation staff has insight into any new routing issues, such as construction and one-way roads.

When selecting a solution to manage your service area maps, look for software that includes simple and user-friendly modification of your maps, as well as GPS receiver functionality that allows you to check in on the quality of the roads your buses use. It should also allow you to easily add way points to change the route driving directions; negating roads traveled to avoid any hazardous or unsafe areas.

Monitor Hazardous or Unsafe Roads

Another factor of maintaining student safety is by avoiding pick-up and drop-off locations near potential dangers such as curves and hills, low-hanging trees, on-street parked cars and snowdrifts. Visibility is a safety issue for the bus driver, other drivers, parents, and even students.

Make sure students are not crossing hazardous roads or walking down roads without sidewalks to get on their bus or when arriving home. These conditions should be monitored in real-time to ensure safe routes.

Ensure Critical Student Data Is Available Any Time

As each school year approaches, you have a small window of time to rollover students and prepare routes for the new year. Accounting for every student's profile and integrating updates and changes is a challenge.

Student data is an incredibly important factor for maintaining safety. Student information including bullying incidents, special needs, medical data, emergency contacts, custody arrangements, and daycare information needs to be updated and accounted for. After, this information needs to be relayed to the necessary people. This critical student data must always be up-to-date and available at any time.

Reduce Walking Distances to Bus Stops

One way to optimize your bus routing is to group students at bus stops for greater efficiency. However, this also means that certain students may have to walk further to reach their bus stops.

A comprehensive safe school bus routing strategy reduces walking distances for students to their stops and keeps track of students with special needs; seeing if they require the bus to stop at their front door. Consider distances between home and school, the age of the students, safe walking routes, and more to determine the best way to reduce walking distances.

Avoid Overloading Buses and Bus Stops

Another factor in safe student transportation is by avoiding the overloading of buses or overcrowding bus stops. Large groups of peers tend to get rowdy together. So, putting together too many different age groups, may incite unnecessary bullying. Strive to create a better balance for student numbers at pick-up and drop-off locations.

Accurately align peers by including information about each student's age when you schedule bus routes. Incidents should always be tracked and kept up to date with other critical student data so that school and transportation staff are aware of any problematic students.

Analyze Bell Times

A big part of efficient bus transportation management is your ability to evaluate bell times to create tiered bus routes. It must be absolutely clear who needs to be where and at what time. You need total insight into bell times and grade levels in order to optimize pick-up times at schools, confirming that your fleet is functioning with the greatest efficiency possible.

We are Here to Help

Orbit Software, Inc. (OSI) works with and consults K-12 school districts on issues pertaining to redistricting and fleet optimization, while accounting for long range school planning.

OSI staff are experts in redistricting, school facility planning and route optimization services. Our staff consists of a perfect combination of skills to provide *School Bus Routing Consulting Services* to K-12 school districts. In addition to consulting, OSI is a leader providing school transportation management software. As new technology arises, OSI strives to incorporate new functionality and features into our process to further enhance the benefits of using our software.

Team project managers of OSI have a combination of over 60 years' experience in school transportation management, GIS analysis, and K-12 school planning. Sonia Mastros has 20+ years of experience in K-12 school transportation management and analytical GIS for school planning. George Mastros possesses 20+ years of software development and K-12 school planning experience. We have met or exceeded every one of our clients' expectations and we strive to maintain that level of service for future clients.

We combine GIS expertise with solid transportation management expertise to provide a team that cannot be matched. OSI has more than adequate capacity to handle a project of any magnitude, in both technology and staff.

Next Step

You will face challenges questioning everything that you have done. Stop questioning yourself. Get to the point that you take responsibility for your actions; be the leader you know you can be. Celebrate the wins and shake off the failures. Tomorrow is a new day.

Where do you see yourself in five or ten years? Aspire to where you want to be, not where you are.

Well for me, I am not sure if I will be retired on the beach somewhere or running for office. I would have never seen myself doing what I am today. I thought I was going to be a schoolteacher with summers off while having a steady paycheck. I would have never thought that I would be in a position of where I had to worry about ensuring other's paychecks.

Uncertainty is frightening, but also exhilarating. Don't be afraid of uncertainty, inspire yourself to keep moving forward. Don't let friends or family decide for you.

Today is the day to take charge of the rest of your life.

If you feel the desire to call, email, or look us up. Do it. Do not let fear get a hold of you.

Visit BusBoss.com

--- Sonia

AUTHOR BIOGRAPHIES

Daisy Oliveras

Daisy comes with a Bachelor's in Business Administration. She graduated in 2009 and moved from Puerto Rico to Pennsylvania and since then, she started working with Orbit Software. She started out as the Receptionist without knowing English. However, eleven years later, she is the Office Manager, raising two beautiful daughters, and has gained so much experience. She likes to help in anyway, whether it be for a co-workers or customers. She is always there for them.

Nicholas Ferrante

Nicholas is a Sales and Marketing Representative at Orbit Software. He graduated from the College of New Jersey with a degree in history and is an avid amateur historian and debater. Before working for Orbit, Nicholas has worked for various companies, usually with a focus on teaching. Begrudgingly residing in New Jersey with his fiancé, Elyssa, Nicholas enjoys a thrilling life of alternating attempting to motivate each of his two overweight cats.

Heather Filer

Heather comes from a strong background in organization, always wanting to try new things. After about 25 years in administration, she decided to completely switch careers and focus on IT and Data Analysis, going back to school and earning eight IT certifications. When she is not cheerfully assisting clients with software issues, you can find her in the woods volunteering at a scout camp or on her couch with a hot cup of tea, blissfully tangled in her yarn.

James Kulp

James has a strong background in technical support and project management. He enjoys helping clients with technical issues, working one on one with clients, while providing training and learning new technology. When he is not assisting clients, you will usually find him blissfully working on his computer or taking a new online course for pleasure and continued learning.

Dana Moyer

Dan has always had an interest in technology, ever since his family bought their first computer. This early love for tech was further fueled by an interest in game design, which led him to study programming, web development and network administration. Acting as one of Orbit Software's technical support specialists, Dan is devoted to ensuring each customer is comfortable and proficient with using our software. Outside of work, Dan can be found building and customizing plastic models, developing mods and maps for video games, drawing, hiking, and playing with his dog.

Sean Long

Sean Long is an Arcadia University graduate with a focus in Computer Science, whom during his studies was also a part of the university's Information Technology, assisting with the daily upkeep of technology services on campus. After graduating, Sean took some time for himself to assist with non-profit or personal programs to help assist his father with his Union Financial Secretary duties. Sean later found a position with Orbit Software starting as a Customer Support Representative. Because his father worked for school transportation contractors and the Berks Area Regional Transportation Association, he was quite familiar with common student/rider transportation practices. He understood the struggles which drivers had when transporting student riders. During this time at Orbit Software, he was able to display his ability to promptly understand software and computer coding practices and worked his way into the Software Developer/Technical Support position he is in now. Outside of work, Sean is actively present in multiple gaming communities offering help or guidance to newcomers to the community who seek it.

George Mastros

George was born in Lancaster, PA but spent most of his childhood near Rome, NY. He got his bachelor's degree in Electrical Engineering from Rochester Institute of Technology.

George has been very active in online forums, primarily teaching others the proper way to deal with Microsoft SQL Server databases. He has been awarded Microsoft SQL Server MVP for eight consecutive years.

George is the VP of Orbit Software and has primarily focused on developing proprietary software that is exclusively owned and sold by Orbit Software, inc. Otherwise, you will find George either cooking amazing meals for his family or out golfing with Sonia.

Sonia Mastros

Sonia is the President and CFO of Orbit Software and knows the value of both education and experience. The challenges of early motherhood and economic hardship as Sonia came of age in her native Puerto Rico led her to earn her own way to a new life with a college degree and the purchase of her own business, Orbit Software.

Life experience taught Sonia the value of education. Her family's entrepreneurial tradition—with both parents and many of her siblings being small business owners—taught Sonia the value of mentorship. And, for years, Sonia successfully maintained her business by drawing on both, in turn. But Sonia wanted more, for herself, for her business, and for her community.

Sonia relished the independence that entrepreneurship provided and saw in her business real potential to impact her community, both as a job creator and as source of mentorship. Sonia's own life had been a journey, and her business a gift.

She wanted to "pay it forward" by growing her business, multiplying job opportunities in her area, and allowing her the opportunity to mentor more employees.

Sonia has been involved with Orbit since its' inception in 1998, during which time, she has personally overseen many projects for various customers from all over the country. Customers ranging from large urban and suburban districts to smaller rural school districts. In all cases, her primary goal was to improve their transportation operations effectively saving the districts money while ensuring student safety.

Sonia is an avid golfer, was the president of her women's golf league and former finance chairperson at her church and knows the value of community involvement.

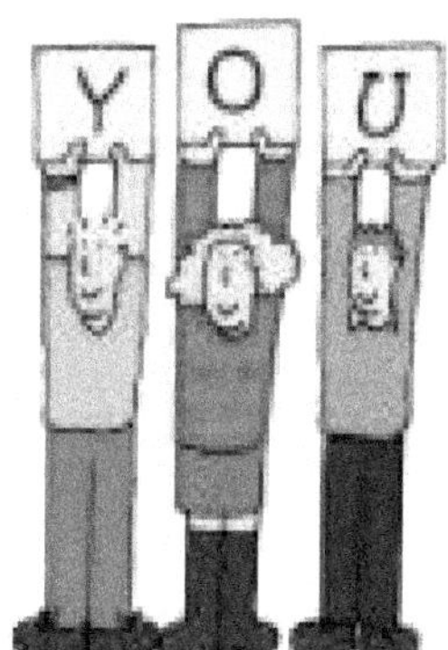

Love this book? Don't forget to leave a review!

Every review matters, and it matters a *lot!*

Head over to Amazon or wherever you purchased this book to leave an honest review for us.

We thank you endlessly.

--- *BusBoss Family*